LIVING WITH PURPOSE

Napoleon Hill (1883–1970), best known for his global bestseller *Think and Grow Rich*, was a self-help author and businessman whose work has influenced millions across the world, from Norman Vincent Peale to Donald Trump. Born poor, Hill lived a colourful life, pursuing several different business ventures and professions. He also met and advised many famous people, such as US President Woodrow Wilson. Hill eventually found widespread success as a motivational author, writing several books on how to achieve success and practically creating the self-help genre.

LIVING WITH PURPOSE

*A Guide to Achieving **Lifelong** Success*

NAPOLEON HILL

RUPA

Published by
Rupa Publications India Pvt. Ltd 2024
7/16, Ansari Road, Daryaganj
New Delhi 110002

Sales centres:
Bengaluru Chennai
Hyderabad Jaipur Kathmandu
Kolkata Mumbai Prayagraj

P-ISBN: 978-93-5702-958-2
E-ISBN: 978-93-5702-778-6

First impression 2024

10 9 8 7 6 5 4 3 2 1

Printed in India

CONTENTS

1

DEFINITENESS OF PURPOSE

It is impressive to recognize that all of the great leaders, in all walks of life and during all periods of history, have attained their leadership by the application of their abilities behind a *definite major purpose.*

It is no less impressive to observe that those who are classified as failures have no such purpose, but they go around and around, like a ship without a rudder, coming back always empty-handed, to their starting point.

Some of these "failures" begin with a definite major purpose but they desert that purpose the moment they are overtaken by temporary defeat or strenuous opposition. They give up and quit, not knowing that there is a philosophy of success which is as dependable and as definite as the rules of mathematics, and never suspecting that temporary defeat is but a testing ground which may prove a blessing in disguise if it is not accepted as final.

Definiteness of purpose and the habit of GOING THE EXTRA MILE constitute a force which staggers the imagination of even the most imaginative of people, although these are but two of the seventeen principles of individual achievement.

These two principles have been here associated for but one purpose. That is to indicate how the principles of this philosophy are blended together like the links of a chain, and how this combination of principles leads to the development of stupendous power which can not be attained by the application singly of any one of them.

THOUGHT BEHIND DEFINITENESS OF PURPOSE

We come now to the analysis of the power of definiteness of purpose and psychological principles from which the power is derived.

First premise: The starting point of all individual achievement is the adoption of a definite purpose and a definite plan for its attainment.

Second premise: All achievement is the result of a motive or combination of motives, of which there are nine basic motives which govern all voluntary actions. (These motives have been previously described.)

Third premise: Any dominating idea, plan or purpose held in the mind, through repetition of thought, and emotionalized with a burning desire for its realization, is taken over by the subconscious section of the mind and acted upon, and it is thus carried through to its logical climax by whatever natural means may be available.

Fourth premise: Any dominating desire, plan or purpose held in the conscious mind and backed by absolute faith in its realization, is taken over and acted upon immediately by the subconscious section of the mind, *and there is no known record of this kind of a desire having ever been without fulfillment.*

Fifth premise: The power of thought is the only thing over which any person has complete, unquestionable control—a fact so astounding that it connotes a close relationship between the mind of man and the Universal Mind of Infinite Intelligence, the connecting link between the two being FAITH.

Sixth premise: The subconscious portion of the mind is the doorway to Infinite Intelligence, and it responds to one's demands in exact proportion to the quality of one's FAITH! The subconscious mind may be reached through faith and given instructions as though it were a person or a complete entity unto itself.

Seventh premise: A definite purpose, backed by absolute faith, is a form of wisdom and wisdom in action produces positive results.

THE MAJOR ADVANTAGES OF DEFINITENESS OF PURPOSE

Definiteness of purpose develops self-reliance, personal initiative, imagination, enthusiasm, self-discipline and concentration of effort, and all of these are prerequisites for the attainment of material success.

It induces one to budget his time and to plan all his day-to-day endeavors so they lead toward the attainment of his MAJOR PURPOSE in life.

It makes one more alert in the recognition of opportunities related to the object of one's MAJOR PURPOSE, and it inspires the necessary courage to act upon those opportunities when they appear.

It inspires the co-operation of other people.

It prepares the way for the full exercise of that state of mind known as FAITH, *by making the mind positive* and freeing it from the limitations of fear and doubt and indecision.

It provides one with a *success consciousness*, without which no one may attain enduring success in any calling.

It destroys the destructive habit of procrastination.

Lastly, it leads directly to the development and the continuous maintenance of the first of the Twelve Riches, a *positive mental attitude.*

These are the major characteristics of DEFINITENESS OF PURPOSE, although it has many other qualities and usages, and it is directly related to each of the Twelve Riches because they are attainable only by singleness of purpose.

Compare the principle of definiteness of purpose with the Twelve Riches, one at a time, and observe how essential it is for the attainment of each.

Then take inventory of the men of outstanding achievement which this country has produced, and observe how each of them has emphasized some major purpose as the object of his endeavors.

HOW TO ACQUIRE A DEFINITE MAJOR PURPOSE

The procedure in the development of a Definite Major Purpose is simple, but important, viz:

(a) Write out a complete, clear and definite statement of your MAJOR PURPOSE IN LIFE, sign it and commit it to memory; then repeat it orally at least once every day, more often if practicable. Repeat it over and over, thus placing back of your purpose all of your faith in Infinite Intelligence.

(b) Write out a clear, definite plan by which you intend to begin the attainment of the object of your DEFINITE MAJOR PURPOSE. In this plan state the maximum time allowed for the attainment of your purpose, and *describe precisely what you intend to give in return for the realization of your purpose,* remembering that there is no such reality as something for nothing, and that everything has a price which must be paid in advance in one form or another.

(c) Make your plan flexible enough to permit changes at any time you are inspired to do so. Remember that Infinite Intelligence, which operates in every atom of matter and in every living or inanimate thing, may present you with a plan far superior to any you can create. Therefore be ready at all times to recognize and adopt any superior plan that may be presented to your mind.

(d) Keep your MAJOR PURPOSE and your plans for attaining it strictly to yourself except insofar as you will receive additional instructions for carrying out your plan, in the description of the MASTER MIND PRINCIPLE, which follows.

MASTER MIND PRINCIPLE

Do not make the mistake of assuming that because you may not understand these instructions the principles here described are not sound. Follow the instructions to the letter; follow them in good faith, and remember that by so doing you are duplicating the procedure of many of the greatest leaders this nation has ever produced.

The instructions call for no effort that you may not easily put forth.

They make no demands upon time or ability with which the average person may not comply.

And they are completely in harmony with the philosophy of all true religions.

Decide *now* what you desire from life and what you have to

give in return. Decide *where* you are going and *how* you are to get there. Then make a start from where you *now* stand. Make the start with whatever means of attaining your goal that may be at hand. And you will discover that to the extent you make use of these, other and better means will reveal themselves to you.

That has been the experience of all men whom the world has recognized as successes. Most of them started with humble beginnings with little more to aid them than a *passionate desire to attain a definite goal.*

There is enduring magic in such a desire!
And lastly, remember:
The Moving Finger writes; and, having writ,
Moves on: nor all thy Piety nor Wit
Shall lure it back to cancel half a Line,
Nor all thy Tears wash out a Word of it.

Yesterday has gone forever! Tomorrow will never arrive, but Today is yesterday's Tomorrow within your reach. What are you doing with it?

Presently I shall reveal to you a principle which is the keystone to the arch of all great achievements; the principle which has been responsible for our great American way of life; our system of free enterprise; our riches and our freedom. But first let us make sure that *you know what it is that you desire of life.*

IDEAS THAT LEAD TO SUCCESS BEGIN AS DEFINITENESS OF PURPOSE

It is a well known fact that ideas are the only assets which have no fixed values. It is equally well known that ideas are the beginning of all achievements.

Ideas form the foundation of all fortunes, the starting point of all inventions. They have mastered the air above us and the waters of the oceans around us; they have enabled us to harness and use the energy known as the ether, through which one brain may communicate with another brain through telepathy.

All ideas begin as the result of Definiteness of Purpose.

The talking machine was nothing but an abstract idea until Edison organized it through definiteness of purpose, and submitted it to the subconscious portion of his brain where it was projected into the great reservoir of Infinite Intelligence, from which a workable plan was flashed back to him. And this workable plan he translated into a machine which worked.

The philosophy of individual achievement began as an idea in the mind of Andrew Carnegie. He backed his idea with definiteness of purpose, and now the philosophy is available for the benefit of millions of people throughout the civilized world.

Moreover, his idea has more than an average chance of becoming one of the great leavening forces of the world, for it is now being used by an ever increasing multitude of people as a means of guiding them through a world of frenzied hysteria in which the spirit of defeatism threatened, for a time, to bring millions of people to a condition of temporary defeat.

The great North American Continent known as the "New World" was discovered and brought under the influence of civilization as the result of an idea which was born in the mind of an humble sailor and backed by definiteness of purpose. And the time is at hand when that idea, born more than four hundred years ago, may lift our nation to a position where it will become the last frontier of civilization, the only hope of human liberty for all mankind.

Any idea that is held in the mind, emphasized, feared or reverenced, begins at once to clothe itself in the most convenient and appropriate physical form that is available.

That which men believe, talk about and fear, whether it be good or bad, has a very definite way of making its appearance in one form or another. Let those who are struggling to free themselves from the limitations of poverty and misery not forget this great truth, for it applies to an individual just as it does to a nation of people.

SELF-SUGGESTION, THE CONNECTING LINK BETWEEN THE CONSCIOUS AND THE SUBCONSCIOUS MIND

Let us now turn our attention to the working principle through which thoughts, ideas, plans, hopes, and purposes which are placed in the conscious mind find their way into the subconscious section of the mind, where they are picked up and carried out to their logical conclusion, through a law of nature which I shall describe later.

To recognize this principle and understand it is to recognize also the reason why Definiteness of Purpose is the beginning of all achievements.

Transfer of thought from the conscious to the subconscious section of the mind may be hastened by the simple process of "stepping up" or stimulating the vibrations of thought through faith, fear, or any other highly intensified emotion, such as enthusiasm, a burning desire based on definiteness of purpose.

Thoughts backed by faith have precedence over all others in the matter of definiteness and speed with which they are handed over to the subconscious section of the mind and are acted upon. The speed with which the power of faith works has given rise to the belief held by many that certain phenomena are the result of "miracles".

Psychologists and scientists recognize no such phenomenon as a miracle, claiming as they do that everything which happens is the result of a definite cause, albeit a cause which cannot be explained. Be that as it may, it is a known fact that the person who is capable of freeing his mind from all self-imposed limitations, through the mental attitude known as faith, generally finds the solution to all of his problems, regardless of their nature.

Psychologists recognize also that Infinite Intelligence, while it is not claimed to be an automatic solver of riddles, nevertheless carries out to a logical conclusion any clearly defined idea, aim, purpose or desire that is submitted to the subconscious section of the mind in a mental attitude of perfect faith.

However, Infinite Intelligence never attempts to modify, change or otherwise alter any thought that is submitted to it, and it has never been known to act upon a mere wish or indefinite idea, thought or purpose. Get this truth well grounded in your mind and you will find yourself in possession of sufficient power to solve your daily problems with much less effort than most people devote to worrying over their problems.

So-called "hunches" often are signals indicating that Infinite Intelligence is endeavoring to reach and influence the conscious section of the mind, but you will observe that they usually come in response to some idea, plan, purpose or desire, or some fear that has been handed over to the subconscious section of the mind.

All "hunches" should be treated civilly and examined carefully, as they often convey, either in whole or in part, information of the utmost value to the individual who receives them. These "hunches" often make their appearance many hours, days or weeks after the thought which inspires them has reached the reservoir of Infinite Intelligence. Meanwhile, the individual often has forgotten the original thought which inspired them.

This is a deep, profound subject about which even the wisest of men know very little. It becomes a self-revealing subject only upon meditation and thought.

Understand the principle of mind operation here described and you will have a dependable clue as to why meditation sometimes brings that which one desires, while at other times it brings that which one does not wish.

This type of mental attitude is attained only by preparation and self-discipline attained through a formula I shall describe later.

It is one of the most profound truths of the world that the affairs of men, whether they are circumstances of mass thought or of individual thought, shape themselves to fit the exact pattern of those thoughts.

Successful men become successful only because they acquire the habit of thinking in terms of success.

Definiteness of purpose can, and it should, so completely occupy the mind *that one has no time or space in the mind for thoughts of failure.*

Another profound truth consists in the fact that the individual who has been defeated and who recognizes himself as a failure may, by reversing the position of the "sails" of his mind, convert the winds of adversity into a power of equal volume which will carry him onward to success, just as,

> One ship sails east, the other west,
> Impelled by the self same blow,
> It's the set of the sails and not the gales,
> That bids them where to go.

To some who pride themselves on being what the world calls "coolheaded, practical business men," this analysis of the principle of Definiteness of Purpose may appear to be abstract or impractical.

There is a power greater than the power of conscious thought, and often it is not perceptible to the finite mind of man. Acceptance of this truth is essential for the successful culmination of any definite purpose based upon the desire for great achievements.

The great philosophers of all ages, from Plato and Socrates on down to Emerson and the moderns, and the great statesmen of our times, from George Washington down to Abraham Lincoln, are known to have turned to the "inner self" in times of great emergency.

We offer no apology for our belief that no great and enduring success has ever been achieved, or ever will be achieved except by those who recognize and use the spiritual powers of the Infinite, as they may be sensed and drawn upon through their "inner selves."

Every circumstance of every man's life is the result of a definite cause, whether it is a circumstance that brings failure or one that brings success.

And most of the circumstances of every man's life are the result of causes over which he has or may have control.

This obvious truth gives importance of the first magnitude to the principle of Definiteness of Purpose. If the circumstances of a man's life are not what he desires he may change them by changing his mental attitude and forming new and more desirable thought habits.

HOW DEFINITENESS OF PURPOSE LEADS TO SUCCESS

Applying the principle of Going The Extra Mile—a principle in which I believe devoutly—I induced the author to permit me to carry out a very important portion of my Definite Major

Purpose in life—that of assisting in taking this philosophy to an ailing world at a time when it is most needed.

I said to the author, as I now say to you, that I would rather have had the privilege of being the author of that philosophy than to have been President of the United States. And next to that I would rather have the privilege of helping to take it to the world, than to own all the world's wealth.

This privilege has been granted me.

And I shall exercise it in a variety of ways. First, I shall make the philosophy available, although in a brief form, through a series of radio programs which will be presented to the people.

Next, I shall help to make the philosophy available in printed lessons which will be distributed to the people through the news stands and book stores of the country.

Then I shall aid in having it interpreted through talking pictures suitable for presentation to the workers in industry, and distributed to them through the co-operation of the management of American Industry.

In addition to these sources of outlet for the philosophy I shall aid in the organization of a nation-wide series of private study clubs in which the philosophy will be presented by talking pictures and through the printed lessons.

It is my purpose to cooperate with the churches of the nation by helping to provide the means by which the philosophy may be made available to their members.

I have also arranged with the author of the philosophy to write a book for children, in which the philosophy will be interpreted in terms that will grip their imagination. This book will be distributed through the book stores and it will be translated into talking pictures for use in the public schools.

Beyond this I hope to make other contributions, as opportunities present themselves, leading to the distribution of this philosophy on a scale so vast that it will become available to every person who is searching for his or her place in the world.

Thus do I have the privilege of revealing the inner workings of a mind that has been inspired with a Definite Major Purpose in life, and though the task may seem extensive, let me assure you that my contribution will be truly a labor of love, and my compensation will consist of an ever increasing reward which is known only to the man who has discovered the blessed privilege of gaining riches by sharing his blessings with others.

Riches—the real riches of life—increase in exact proportion to the scope and extent of the benefit they bring to those with whom they are shared. I know this to be true for I have grown rich by sharing. I have never benefitted anyone in any manner whatsoever without having received in return, from one source or another, ten times as much benefit as I have contributed to others.

In sharing my riches with others, I seek no glorification, for my benefactions are made anonymously except in rare instances when my identity must be revealed. Instead of seeking glorification of my name, I prefer to glorify my soul through useful service to others. The riches I give away add to my own estate in Happy Valley.

I wish no monuments built to my name after I am gone. I prefer rather to build my own monuments while I live, in the hearts of my fellowmen—not monuments to my name, but monuments to the spirit of Fellowship which I am endeavoring to promote for the good of mankind.

In this spirit I have created the great estate of Happy Valley; in this spirit I shall maintain the estate as long as I live.

And this is the spirit which I recommend to you who are seeking the path to Happy Valley.

You will find that path most quickly by helping others to find it.

One of the strangest of all truths which have been revealed to me is the fact that the surest way to solve one's personal problems is to find someone with a greater problem and help him to solve it, through some method of application of the habit of Going The Extra Mile.

This is a simple formula, but it has charm and magic, and it never fails to work.

However, you cannot appropriate the formula by the mere acceptance of my testimony as to its soundness. You must adopt it and apply it in your own way. You will then need no testimony as to its soundness.

You will find that many opportunities surround you.

The destruction wrought by World War II has bewildered and frustrated many millions of people who are now searching for the path to Happy Valley. They need only a spark of human kindness to give them new hope and the courage to carry on. You can supply that spark to those nearest you.

By helping others to find the path *you will find it for yourselves!*

You might begin by organizing a Fellowship Club among your own neighbors or fellow workers, casting yourself for the role of leader and teacher of the group.

Here you will learn another great truth, namely, that the best way to appropriate the principles of the philosophy of individual achievement is by teaching it to others. When a man begins to teach anything he begins also to learn more about that which he is teaching.

You are now a student of this philosophy, but you can become a master of it by teaching it to others. Thus your compensation will be assured you in advance.

If you are a worker in industry here is your big opportunity to find yourself by helping others to adjust their relationships in peace and harmony. For soundness it has never been excelled, for it has been fully verified by the experiences of men in every walk of life.

Labor does not need agitators, but it does need peacemakers. It also needs a sound philosophy for the guidance of its following—a philosophy that benefits both the management and the workers. To this end the principles of this philosophy are perfectly suited.

The labor leader who guides his followers by this philosophy will have the *confidence of his followers and the fullest cooperation of their employers.* Is that not obvious? Is it not sufficient promise of reward to justify the adoption of this philosophy?

A labor organization conducted by the principles of this philosophy would benefit everyone whom it affected. Friction would be supplanted by harmony in human relationships. Agitators and exploiters of labor would be automatically eliminated. The funds of the labor organization could be used for the education of its members and not for political intrigues.

And there would be more profits for distribution as wages—*profits which the management of industry would prefer to give to their workers instead of being forced to use them as a defense fund against the destructive efforts of agitators.*

There is a need for a Fellowship Club in every industry.

In the larger industries there is room for many such clubs.

The membership should consist of both the workers and the management, for here is a common meeting ground based upon principles on which everyone could agree. And agreement here would mean agreement at the workbench or the lathe.

I have emphasized this particular field of opportunity because I recognize that the chaos existing in the relationship between the management of industry and the workers constitutes *the number one economic problem of this nation.*

If you have not already adopted a Definite Major Purpose in life here is an opportunity for you to do so. You can start right where you are, by helping to teach this philosophy to those who are in need of it.

The time has come when it is not only beneficial to the individual to help his neighbor to solve his personal problems, *but it is imperative that each of us do so as a means of self-preservation.*

If your neighbor's house were on fire you would volunteer to help him put out the fire, even if you were not on friendly terms with him, for common sense would convince you that this would be the means of saving your own house.

In recommending harmony between the management of industry and the workers, I am not thinking of the interests of management alone, for I recognize that if this harmony does not prevail there soon will be *neither management nor workers as we know them today.*

On the other hand, the man with a sound philosophy of life will find himself surrounded with an abundance of opportunities such as did not exist a decade ago.

The man who tries to get ahead without a Definite Major Purpose will meet with difficulties far greater than the average man can master.

The more lucrative opportunities of the world of today and tomorrow will go to those who prepare themselves for leadership in their chosen calling.

And leadership in any field of endeavor requires a foundation of sound philosophy. The days of the "hit and miss" leadership are gone forever. Skill and technique and human understanding will be required in the changed world we are now approaching.

The foremen and supervisors in industry must take on new responsibilities in the future. They must not only be skilled in the mechanics of their jobs, which is so essential for efficient production, but they must be skilled as well in the production of harmony among the workers for whom they are responsible.

The youngsters of today will become the leaders of our society tomorrow. What are we going to do about them? This is a problem of the first magnitude, and the major portion of the burden of solving it will fall upon the shoulders of the teachers in the public schools.

I mention these obvious facts as evidence that the future holds forth opportunities for useful service such as we have never known before; opportunities born of necessity in a world which has changed so rapidly that some fail to recognize the scope and the nature of the changes which have taken place.

Take inventory, you who are without a Definite Major Purpose; to find out where you fit in this changed world; prepare yourselves for your new opportunities and make the most of them.

If I had the privilege of so doing I could no doubt choose for you a Definite Major Purpose suited in every way to your qualifications and needs, and I might create for you a simple plan by which you could attain the object of that purpose; but I can serve you more profitably by teaching you how to do this for yourself.

Somewhere along the way the idea for which you are searching will reveal itself to you. That has been the experience of most of the students of this philosophy. When the idea comes you will recognize it, for it should come with such force that you cannot escape it. You may be sure of that provided you are sincerely searching for it.

One of the imponderable features of this philosophy is that it inspires the creation of new ideas, reveals the presence of opportunities for self-advancement which had been previously overlooked, and inspires one to move on his own personal initiative in embracing and making the most of such opportunities.

This feature of the philosophy is not the result of chance. It was designed to produce a specific effect, since it is obvious that an opportunity which a man creates for himself, or an idea with which he may be inspired through his own thought, is more beneficial than any he may borrow from others, for the very procedure by which a man creates useful ideas leads him unerringly to the discovery of the source from which he may acquire additional ideas when he needs them.

While it is of great benefit to a man to have access to a source from which he may receive the inspiration necessary to create his own ideas, and self-reliance is an asset of priceless value, there may come a time when he will need to draw upon the resources of other minds. And that time is sure to come to those who aspire to leadership in the higher brackets of personal achievement.

Presently I shall reveal to you the means by which personal power may be attained, through the consolidation of many minds directed to the achievement of definite ends.

It was by this same means that Andrew Carnegie ushered in the great steel age and gave America its greatest industry, although he had no capital with which to begin, and very little education.

And it was by this means that Thomas A. Edison became the greatest inventor of all times, although he had no personal knowledge of physics, mathematics, chemistry, electronics or many other scientific subjects, all of which were essential in his work as an inventor.

It should give you hops to know that lack of education, lack of working capital, and lack of technical skill need not discourage you from establishing, as your major goal in life, any purpose you may choose, for this philosophy provides a way by which any goal within reason may be attained by any man of average ability.

The one thing it cannot do for you is to choose your goal for you!

But, once you have established your own goal, this philosophy can guide you unerringly to its attainment. That is a promise without qualifications.

We cannot tell you what to desire, or how much success to hope for, but we can and we shall reveal to you the formula by which successes may be attained.

Your major responsibility right now is to find out what you desire in life, where you are going, and what you will do when you get there. This is one responsibility which no one but you can assume, and it is a responsibility ninety-eight out of every hundred people never assume. *That is the major reason why only two out of every hundred people can be rated as successful.*

Success begins through Definiteness of Purpose!

If this fact has seemed to be over-emphasized it is because of the common trait of procrastination which influences ninety-eight out of every hundred people to go all the way through life without choosing a Definite Major Purpose.

Singleness of purpose is a priceless asset—priceless because so few possess it.

Yet it is an asset which one may appropriate on a second's notice.

Make up your mind what you desire of life, decide to get just that, without substitutes, and lo! you will have taken possession of one of the most priceless of all assets available to human beings.

But your desire must be no mere wish or hope!

It must be a *burning desire*, and it must become so definitely an obsessional desire that you are willing to pay whatever price its attainment may cost. The price may be much or it may be little, but you must condition your mind to pay it, regardless of what the cost may be.

The moment you choose your Definite Major Purpose in life you will observe a strange circumstance, consisting in the fact that ways and means of attaining that purpose will begin immediately to reveal themselves to you.

Opportunities you had not expected will be placed in your way.

The cooperation of others will become available to you, and friends will appear as if by a stroke of magic. Your fears and doubts will begin to disappear and self-reliance will take their place.

This may seem, to the uninitiated, a fantastic promise, but not so to the man who has done away with indecision and has chosen a definite goal in life. I speak not from the observation of other men alone, but from my own personal experience. I have transformed myself from a dismal failure to an outstanding success, and I have therefore earned the right to give you this assurance of what you may expect if you follow the road-map provided by this philosophy.

When you come to that inspiring moment when you choose your Definite Major Purpose, do not become discouraged if relatives or friends who are nearest you call you a "dreamer."

Just remember that the dreamers have been the forerunners of all human progress.

They have given us the great American system of free enterprise.

They have given us our greatest asset, the privilege of enjoying personal liberty and the right to dream when we choose.

They have given us the greatest air force and the greatest navy in the world.

They have pushed back the frontiers of civilization and have made of the American way of life a glorious pattern which is the envy of the rest of the world.

Christopher Columbus dreamed of an unknown world, set sail on an uncharted ocean and discovered a new world.

Copernicus dreamed of an unseen world, and with the aid of an improvised telescope revealed it, thus setting civilization ahead ten thousand years in the mastery of fear and superstition.

Thomas A. Edison dreamed of a lamp that could be lighted by electricity, went to work on his dream, and despite the fact that he met with ten thousand failures he gave the world that lamp.

So, let no one discourage you from dreaming, but make sure you back your dreams with action based on Definiteness of Purpose. Your chances for success are as great as have been those of anyone who has preceded you. In many ways your chances are greater, for you now have access to the knowledge of the principles of individual achievement which millions of successful men of the past had to acquire the long and hard way.

Wise men share most of their riches generously. They share their confidences sparingly, and take great care not to misplace them. And when they talk of their aims and plans they generally do it by *action* rather than by words.

Wise men listen much and speak with caution, for they know that a man may always be in the way of learning something of value when he is listening, while he may learn nothing when he is speaking, unless it be the folly of *talking too much!*

There is always an appropriate time for one to speak and an appropriate time for one to remain silent. Wise men, when in doubt as to whether to speak or remain silent, give themselves the benefit of the doubt by keeping quiet.

Exchange of thought, through intercourse of speech, is one of the more important means by which men gather useful knowledge, create plans for the attainment of their Definite Major Purpose and find ways and means of carrying out these plans. And the "round table" discussions are an outstanding feature among men in the higher brackets of achievement. But these are far different from the idle discussions in which some men open their minds to anyone who wishes to enter.

Presently I shall reveal to you a safe method by which you may exchange thoughts with other men, with a reasonable assurance that you will *get* as much as you *give,* or more. By this method you may not only speak freely of your most cherished plans, but it will be profitable for you to so do.

I shall reveal to you an important intersection at which you may leave the by-path you are following on your way to Happy Valley, and get on the main highway! The way will be clearly marked so that you shall not miss it.

This intersection of which I speak is the point at which men in the higher brackets of achievement come to a parting of the ways with many of their former associates and confidants, and join company with men who are prepared to give them a lift on their journey to Happy Valley.

POINTS TO REMEMBER

1. The starting point of all individual achievement is the adoption of a definite purpose.
2. There are nine basic motives which govern all voluntary actions.
3. Destroy the destructive habit of procrastination.

2

APPLIED FAITH

If you had a definite major purpose, knew exactly what you wanted to do, had a mastermind alliance of people that could help you do it, and then had the sufficient faith to keep you going while you did it, that would be about all you would need.

Why do you suppose we need the fourteen additional principles? We need fourteen additional principles to induce you to make use of these three.

You need personal initiative. You need imagination. You need enthusiasm. In other words, this philosophy is like baking a cake. When you bake a cake, you don't put in just one ingredient. You put in a pinch of this, a pinch of that, a dash of the other thing, and then you put it in the stove and bake it. If you took out any one of those ingredients, you wouldn't end up with the same kind of cake. It's the same way with this philosophy. You can't leave out any one of these seventeen principles. It would be like taking a link out of a chain. You wouldn't have a chain anymore, you'd have two parts of a chain, but not a whole chain. The other fourteen principles are supporting principles of these three.

Faith is a state of mind that has been called the mainspring of the soul, to which one's aims, desires, plans, and purposes may be translated into their physical or financial equivalent.

There are the fundamentals of faith, but by applied faith, I'm talking about something vastly different from mere belief. The word *applied* means what? Action. It's the action part of faith. Without action, faith is nothing but just daydreaming. There are a lot of people who believe in things but don't do anything about them, engaging only in daydreaming. Applied faith is an active faith.

FAITH AND THE FIRST THREE PRINCIPLES OF SUCCESS

1. **Definiteness of Purpose.** Purpose is supported by a personal initiative and action, action, action—the more action, the better. That means continual action, not only on your part but also on the part of those that may be cooperating with you or your mastermind allies.
2. **Positive Mental Attitude.** A positive mind, free from all negatives such as fear, envy, hatred, jealousy, and greed, is essential. Mental attitude determines the effectiveness of faith. It's a fact. The frame of mind that you are in when you pray will determine what happens as a result of that prayer. There's no two ways about it. You can test it for yourself and find out.

   I have no doubt that you have had the experiences that I've had, sending out prayers that didn't produce anything but a negative result. Do you suppose there is anybody that *didn't* have that experience at one time or another? When you pray, unless you have such absolute faith that whatever you are going after you're going to acquire, and that you can see it in advance in your possession before you start asking for it, chances are the effect of your prayer is going to be negative.

3. **Mastermind Alliance.** A mastermind alliance convenes one or more other people who radiate courage based on faith and are suited mentally and spiritually to one's needs in carrying out a given purpose.

ELEMENTS OF APPLIED FAITH

1. **Every adversity carries with it the seed of an equivalent benefit; temporary defeat is not failure until it has been accepted as such.** Do you know where the majority of people fall down in connection with their application of their faith? It's when they're defeated and they accept that defeat as being something they can't do anything about. Instead of beginning immediately to search for that seed of an equivalent benefit that's in *every* defeat, they become moody and broody, discouraged, and build up inferiority complexes. Instead, they could reverse the order and *use* defeat as nothing more than a temporary point from which to make another effort.

My saying that every adversity carries with it the seed of an equivalent benefit, that every defeat and every failure carries the seed of an equivalent benefit, wouldn't mean anything to you unless I made application of it, and gave you illustration after illustration. If you examine enough illustrations in your own experience, you'll see that it always works out that way. That's why I want you to look closely at the adversities that come to you.

Do you know that your adversities are often your greatest blessings? Do you know the greatest blessing that ever came into my life? Of course, it was the loss of my mother.

Ordinarily, the greatest catastrophe that could overtake a child would be to lose his mother at the age of nine years.

Why do I say that was the greatest, greatest blessing? Because it brought me a new mother to take her place, one who is responsible for everything that I've achieved and everything that I shall achieve. Without her influence, I'd still be fighting rattlesnakes, drinking mountain liquor, and fighting feuds. My relatives are still doing that same thing, so there's no reason to expect that I wouldn't be. I've had a lot of other adversities, and I want to tell you that without some twenty major adversities I've gone through, I would never have been able to pursue the soundness of this philosophy—that there is a seed of equivalent benefit in every adversity.

Can you imagine any worse adversity to a man than to be informed that his son was born without any signs of ears and would be a deaf and dumb mute all of his life? Can you imagine anything worse than that? I'll always be thankful that because of my contact with Infinite Intelligence, my deaf son was provided with a sort of hearing system that gave him 65 percent of his normal hearing and eventually 100 percent with a modern hearing aid. He learned to live a normal life and I got the greatest demonstration of my entire experience in the power of faith. I couldn't have gotten it any other way. I couldn't have gotten it secondhand, I had to get it firsthand.

I never accepted that affliction of that child, not even before I saw him, and not even after I saw him. I never accepted it. His relatives accepted it. They wanted to put him in the school of underprivileged where he'd learn sign language and lip reading. I didn't even want him to know there *were* such things. When he was old enough to go to school, I had a fight with the school authorities every year just as regular as a clock, because they wanted to send him to a school for underprivileged children, to mix with the other children and see their afflictions. I didn't want him to know there were such things. I taught him from the very beginning that his not having any ears was a great blessing—and he believed it. Compassion led people to do things for him they wouldn't have done otherwise. He got a job as a salesman for the *Saturday Evening Post* and he led every salesman throughout the United States. He'd often go out with five dollars' worth of merchandise and come back with ten dollars in cash. He did that many times. People would look at him and say, "Why that poor little fellow with no ears is out selling papers. I guess his parents are poor." They'd give him a dollar bill and when he'd try to give them their change, they'd say, "Oh, sonny, you just keep that." So he'd often get a dollar apiece for the *Saturday Evening Post.* Not at all conscious today of any affliction, he's living a perfectly normal life because I taught him that an affliction, *any kind of an affliction,* can be transmuted into a benefit.

2. **Applied faith requires the habit of affirming one's definite major purpose in the form of a prayer at least once daily.** The subconscious mind only knows what you tell it, or what you allow other people to tell it, or what you allow the circumstances of life to tell it. It doesn't know the difference between a lie and the truth. It doesn't know the difference between a penny and a million dollars. It accepts the things that you send over, and if you send over predominating thoughts on poverty and ill health and failure, that's exactly what'll you get. No matter how much faith that you may have later on, you'll find out the subconscious responds to the mental attitude that you're maintaining during the day. It's necessary for you to affirm over and over again the objects that you are going to attain in life until you educate your subconscious mind to automatically attract to you the things that are related

to what you're aiming to attain in life. You'll find that your mind is like an electrode magnet and once you charge it with a clear picture of what you want, it'll attract to you from the highways and the byways the things that you need to carry out that purpose.

3. **Recognition of the existence of an Infinite Intelligence that gives order to the vast, entire universe**. You are a minute expression of this intelligence and as such your mind has no limitation except those accepted or set up in your own mind. Let me repeat that statement. Your mind has no limitations whatsoever, except those that you allow to be established there or that you deliberately set up in your mind or accept. That's a pretty broad statement. However, the achievements of men like Mr. Edison, Mr. Ford, Mr. Carnegie, and Napoleon Hill (if you please) definitely support the idea that there is no limitation except that which you set up in your mind.

If I had ever wavered for one second in my belief of what I would do, from the time that I started with Mr. Carnegie up until the time I gave this philosophy to the world, I would never have done it. How did I do it? Do you have any idea what played the strongest part in what I've achieved? It wasn't my brilliancy and it wasn't my outstanding intelligence. I have no more brilliance than the average person and no more intelligence than the average person. But, I believed that I could do it and I never stopped believing it. The harder the going was, the more I believed I would do it. If you can take that attitude toward yourself, throwing yourself over on the side of yourself when you're overtaken by adversity, or when people are against you, and not go *against* yourself, then you're using applied faith.

You've got to do that.

Do you know there are testing times for people? Nobody is permitted to attain a high state in life and stay there without being tested. Nobody is allowed to go into a well-managed business or go to a high position and stay there without being tested at lower positions until, step-by-step, he earns the right to be up on the top. I don't know how the Creator runs his business entirely, but I can catch a pretty good idea of how he does it from observing that part which I can understand. Of course, there's much more that I *can't* understand, but I can definitely see that he allows nobody to attain to a higher stage of life without giving him severe testing.

One of the most outstanding things that I found in my research was that the men of great achievement in all walks of life, and throughout the ages, were great only in proportion as they had been defeated and as they met with opposition. What an outstanding thing. It couldn't be a coincidence that every one of these outstanding men was exactly great in proportion as he had been small and as he had been opposed and as he had had to struggle.

I used to tell of my early struggles and tell some of my defeats. My business manager said it wasn't a good idea. I think it's a fine idea, because if you knew the amount of the major defeats that I have met, recognizing how I still kept my head above water and still live to deliver this philosophy, you'd say, "If Hill can do it, I can do it too." That's the only reason I ever spoke of it.

I don't mind what terms you use: God, Jehovah, Buddha, or Muhammad. You can call it anything you want to. No matter what you call it, we're all talking about one first cause. There aren't two first causes, there's only one. There couldn't be two. There's one first cause that's responsible for this great universe we're living in—for you and for me and for everything that's in the universe. I call it Infinite Intelligence because I have students of all faiths and all religions all over the world and Infinite Intelligence happens to be a neutral term nobody can object to.

But unless you not only believe in that, unless you can prove to yourself, and absolutely put down on paper evidence that there is first cause that you can draw upon, you're not going to be able to make the fullest use of a definite plan.

One of my students asked me about my concept of Infinite Intelligence and if I meant the same thing as God. I said, "Yes I do." "Well," he said, "can you prove the existence of your concept of God?" I replied, "Everything in the universe is the finest evidence of Its existence, because of the orderliness of the universe." Everything's orderly, from the electrons and protons in the smallest part of the matter, up to the largest suns that float through the heavens. Everything's in orderliness: no chaos, no running together of the planets. There's more evidence of a first cause than there is of anything that I know of. And, if you don't believe that, if you don't accept it, if you don't see it, if you don't feel it, and if you don't know it, then you won't know that you are a minute part of that Infinite Intelligence being expressed through your brain. If you recognize that, then you recognize the truth of what I said—that your only limitations are those which you set up in your mind, or permit somebody to set up there, or let circumstances establish there for you.

Careful inventory of your past defeats (and adversities from it) shows that all such experiences do carry the seed of an equivalent benefit.

POINTS TO REMEMBER

1. Without action, faith is nothing but just daydreaming.
2. *Any kind of an affliction,* can be transmuted into a benefit.
3. You'll find that your mind is like an electrode magnet and once you charge it with a clear picture of what you want, it'll attract to you the things that you need.

3

GOLDEN RULE

There is more power wrapped up in the preceding lessons of this course than most men could trust themselves with; therefore, this lesson is a governor that will, if observed and applied, enable you to steer your ship of knowledge over the rocks and reefs of failure that usually beset the pathway of all who come suddenly into possession of power.

For more than twenty-five years I have been observing the manner in which men behave themselves when in possession of power, and I have been forced to the conclusion that the man who attains it in any other than by the slow, step-by-step process, is constantly in danger of destroying himself and all whom he influences.

It must have become obvious to you, long before this, that this entire course leads to the attainment of *power* of proportions which may be made to perform the seemingly "impossible." Happily, it becomes apparent that this power can only be attained by the observance of many fundamental principles all of which converge in this lesson, which is based upon a law that both equals and transcends in importance every other law outlined in the preceding lessons.

Likewise, it becomes apparent to the thoughtful student that this *power* can endure only by faithful observance of the law upon which this lesson is based, wherein lies the "safety-valve" that protects the careless student from the dangers of his own follies; and protects, also, those whom he might endanger if he tried to circumvent the injunction laid down in this lesson.

To "prank" with the power that may be attained from the knowledge wrapped up in the preceding lessons of this course, without a full understanding and strict observance of the law laid down in this lesson, is the equivalent of "pranking" with a power which may destroy as well as create.

I am speaking, now, not of that which I suspect to be true, but, of that which I KNOW TO BE TRUE! The truth upon which this entire course, and this lesson in particular, is founded, is no invention of mine. I lay no claim to it except that of having observed its unvarying application in the everyday walks of life over a period of more than twenty-five years of struggle; and, of having appropriated as much of it as, in the light of my human frailties and weaknesses, I could make use of.

If you demand *positive* proof of the soundness of the laws upon which this course in general, and this lesson in particular, is founded, I must plead inability to offer it except through one witness, and that is *yourself.*

You may have *positive* proof only by testing and applying these laws for yourself.

If you demand more substantial and authoritative evidence than my own, then I am privileged to refer you to the teachings and philosophy of Christ, Plato, Socrates, Epictetus, Confucius,

Emerson and two of the more modern philosophers, James and Münsterberg, from whose works I have appropriated all that constitutes the more important fundamentals of this lesson, with the exception of that which I have gathered from my own limited experience.

For more than four thousand years men have been preaching

the Golden Rule as a suitable rule of conduct among men, but unfortunately the world bas accepted the letter while totally missing the spirit of this Universal Injunction. We have accepted the Golden Rule philosophy merely as a sound rule of ethical conduct but we have failed to understand the law upon which it is based.

I have heard the Golden Rule quoted scores of times, but I do not recall having ever heard an explanation of the law upon which it is based, and not until recent years did I understand that law, from which I am led to believe that those who quoted it did not understand it.

The Golden Rule means, substantially, to do unto others as you would wish them to do unto you if your positions were reversed.

But why? What is the *real* reason for this kindly consideration of others?

The real reason is this:

There is an eternal law through the operation of which we reap that which we sow. When you select the rule of conduct by which you guide yourself in your transactions with others, you will be fair and just, very likely, if you know that you are setting into motion, by that selection, a *power* that will run its course for weal or woe in the lives of others, returning, finally, to help or to hinder you, according to its nature.

"Whatsoever a man soweth that shall he also reap"!

It is your privilege to deal unjustly with others, but, if you understand the law upon which the Golden Rule is based, you must know that your unjust dealings will "come home to roost."

You cannot pervert or change the course of this law, *but you can adapt yourself to its nature and thereby use it as an irresistible power that will carry you to heights of achievement which could not be attained without its aid.*

This law does not stop by merely flinging back upon you your acts of injustice and unkindness toward others; it goes further than this—much further—and returns to you the results of every *thought* that you release.

Therefore, not alone is it advisable to "do unto others as you wish them to do unto you," but to avail yourself fully of the benefits of this great Universal Law you must "think of others as you wish them to think of you."

The law upon which the Golden Rule is based begins affecting you, either for good or evil, the moment you release a *thought.* It has amounted almost to a worldwide tragedy that people have not generally understood this law. Despite the simplicity of the law it is practically all there is to be learned that is of enduring value to man, for it is the medium through which we become the masters of our own destiny.

Understand this law and you understand *all* that the Bible has to unfold to you, for the Bible presents one unbroken chain of evidence in support of the fact that man is the maker of his own destiny; and, that his *thoughts* and *acts* are the tools with which he does the *making.*

During ages of less enlightenment and tolerance than that of the present, some of the greatest thinkers the world has ever produced have paid with their lives for daring to uncover this Universal Law so that it might be understood by all. In the light of the past history of the world, it is an encouraging bit of evidence, in support of the fact that men are gradually throwing off the veil of ignorance and intolerance, to note that I stand in no danger of bodily harm for writing that which would have cost me my life a few centuries ago.

◆

While this course deals with the highest laws of the universe, which man is capable of interpreting, the aim, nevertheless, has been to show how these laws may be used in the practical affairs of life. With this object of practical application in mind, let us now proceed to analyze the effect of the Golden Rule through the following incident.

THE POWER OF PRAYER

"No," said the lawyer, "I shan't press your claim against that man; you can get someone else to take the case, or you can withdraw it; just as you please."

"Think there isn't any money in it?"

"There probably would be some little money in it, but it would come from the sale of the little house that the man occupies and calls his home! But I don't want to meddle with the matter, anyhow."

"Got frightened out of it, eh?"

"Not at all."

"1 suppose likely the fellow begged hard to be let off?"

"Well, yes, he did."

"And you caved in, likely?"

"Yes."

"What in creation did you do?"

"I believe I shed a few tears."

"And the old fellow begged you hard, you say?"

"No, I didn't say so; he didn't speak a word to me."

"Well, may I respectfully inquire whom he did address in your hearing?"

"God Almighty."

"Ah, he took to praying, did he?"

"Not for my benefit, in the least. You see, I found the little house easily enough and knocked on the outer door, which stood ajar; but nobody heard me, so I stepped into the little hall and saw through the crack of a door a cozy sitting-room, and there on the bed, with her silver head high on the pillows, was an old lady who looked for all the world just like my mother did the last time I ever saw her on earth. Well, I was on the point of knocking, when she said: 'Come, father, now begin; I'm all ready.' And down on his knees by her side went an old, white-haired man, still older than his wife, I should judge, and I couldn't have knocked then, for the life of me. Well, he began. First, he reminded God they were still His submissive children, mother and he, and no matter what He saw fit to bring upon them they shouldn't rebel at His will. Of course 'twas going to be very hard for them to go out homeless in their old age, especially with poor mother so sick and helpless, and, oh! how different it all might have been if only one of the boys had been spared. Then his voice kind of broke, and a white hand stole from under the coverlet and moved softly over his snowy hair. Then he went on to repeat that nothing could be so sharp again as the parting with those three sons—unless mother and he should be separated.

"But, at last, he fell to comforting himself with the fact that the dear Lord knew that it was through no fault of his own that mother and he were threatened with the loss of their dear little home, which meant beggary and the alms-house—a place they prayed to be delivered from entering if it should be consistent with God's will. And then he quoted a multitude of promises concerning the safety of those who put their trust in the Lord. In fact, it was the most thrilling plea to which I ever listened. And at last, he prayed for God's blessing on those who were about to demand justice."

The lawyer then continued, more lowly than ever: "And I—

believe—I'd rather go to the poor-house myself tonight than to stain my heart and hands with the blood of such a prosecution as that."

"Little afraid to defeat the old man's prayer, eh?"

"Bless your soul, man, you couldn't defeat it!" said the lawyer. "I tell you he left it all subject to the will of God; but he claimed that we were told to make known our desires unto God; but of all the pleadings I ever heard that beat all. You see, I was taught that kind of thing myself in my childhood. Anyway, why was I sent to bear that prayer? I am sure I don't know, but I hand the case over."

"I wish," said the client, twisting uneasily, "you hadn't told me about the old man's prayer."

"Why so?"

"Well, because I want the money the place would bring; but I was taught the Bible straight enough when I was a youngster and I'd hate to run counter to what you tell about. I wish you hadn't heard a word about it, and, another time, I wouldn't listen to petitions not intended for my ears."

The lawyer smiled.

"My dear fellow," he said, "you're wrong again. It was intended for my ears, and yours, too; and God Almighty intended it. My old mother used to sing about God's moving in a mysterious way, as I remember it."

"Well, my mother used to sing it, too," said the claimant, as he twisted the claim-papers in his fingers.

"You can call in the morning, if you like, and tell 'mother' and 'him' the claim has been met."

"In a mysterious way," added the lawyer, smiling.

Neither this lesson nor the course of which it is a part is based upon an appeal to maudlin sentiment, but there can be no escape from the truth that *success*, in its highest and noblest form, brings one, finally, to view all human relationships with a feeling of deep emotion such as that which this lawyer felt when he overheard the old man's prayer.

If may be an old-fashioned idea, but somehow I can't get away from the belief that *no man can attain success in its highest form without the aid of earnest prayer!*

Prayer is the key with which one may open the secret doorway. In this age of mundane affairs, when the uppermost thought of the majority of people is centered upon the accumulation of wealth, or the struggle for a mere existence, it is both easy and natural for us to overlook the power of earnest prayer.

I am not saying that you should resort to prayer as a means of solving your daily problems which press for immediate attention; no, I am not going that far in a course of instruction which will be studied largely by those who are seeking in it the road to *success* that is measured in dollars; but, may I not modestly suggest to *you* that you, at least, give *prayer* a trial after *everything else fails* to bring you a *satisfying success?*

Thirty men, red-eyed and disheveled, lined up before the judge of the San Francisco police court. It was the regular morning company of drunks and disorderlies. Some were old and hardened; others hung their heads in shame. Just as the momentary disorder attending the bringing in of the prisoners quieted down, a strange thing happened. A strong, clear voice from below began singing:

"Last night I lay a-sleeping,
There came a dream so fair."

"Last night!" It had been for them all a nightmare or a drunken stupor. The song was such a contrast to the horrible fact that no one could fail of a sudden shock at the thought the song suggested.

"I stood in old Jerusalem,
Beside the Temple there,"

The song went on. The judge had paused. He made a quiet inquiry. A former member of a famous opera company known all over the country was awaiting trial for forgery. It was he who was singing in his cell.

Meantime the song went on, and every man in the line showed emotion. One or two dropped on their knees; one boy at the end of the line, after a desperate effort at self-control, leaned against the wall, buried his face against his folded arms, and sobbed, "Oh, mother, mother."

The sobs, cutting to the very heart the men who heard, and the song, still welling its way through the court-room, blended in the hush. At length one man protested. "Judge," said he, "have we got to submit to this? We're here to take our punishment, but this—" He, too, began to sob.

It was impossible to proceed with the business of the court; yet the court gave no order to stop the song. The police sergeant, after an effort to keep the men in line, stepped back and waited with the rest. The song moved on to its climax:

"Jerusalem, Jerusalem!
Sing, for the night is o'er!
Hosanna, in the highest!
Hosanna, for evermore!"

In an ecstasy of melody the last words rang out, and then there was silence. The judge looked into the faces of the men before him. There was not one who was not touched by the song; not one in whom some better impulse was not stirred. He did not call the cases singly—a kind word of advice, and he dismissed them all. No man was fined or sentenced to the workhouse that morning. The song had done more good than *punishment* could possibly have accomplished.

You have read the story of a Golden Rule lawyer and a Golden Rule judge. In these two commonplace incidents of everyday life you have observed how the Golden Rule works when *applied.*

A passive attitude toward the Golden Rule will bring no results; it is not enough merely to *believe* in the philosophy, while, at the same time, failing to *apply* it in your relationships with others. If you want results you must take an *active* attitude toward the Golden Rule. A mere passive attitude, represented by belief in its soundness, will avail you nothing.

Nor will it avail you anything to proclaim to the world your belief in the Golden Rule while your actions are not in harmony with your proclamation. Conversely stated, it will avail you nothing to appear to practice the Golden Rule, while, at heart, you are willing and eager to use this universal law of right conduct as a cloak to cover up a covetous and selfish nature. Murder will out. Even the most ignorant person will "sense" you for what you are.

> Human character does evermore publish itself. It will not be concealed. It hates darkness—it rushes into light... I heard an experienced counselor say that he never feared the effect upon a jury of a lawyer who does not believe in his heart that his client ought to have a verdict. If he does not believe it, his unbelief will appear to the jury, despite all his protestations, and will become their unbelief. This is that law whereby a work of art, of whatever kind, sets us in the same state of mind wherein the artist was when he made it. That which we do not believe we cannot *adequately say,* though we may repeat the words ever so

> often. It was this conviction which Swedenborg expressed when he described a group of persons in the spiritual world endeavoring in vain to articulate a proposition which they did not believe; but they could not, though they twisted and folded their lips even to indignation.
>
> A man passes for what he is worth. What he is engraves itself on his face, on his form, on his fortunes, in letters of light which all men may read but himself... If you would not be known to do anything, never do it. A man may play the fool in the drifts of a desert, but every grain of sand shall seem to see.
>
> —Emerson.

It is the law upon which the Golden Rule philosophy is based to which Emerson has reference in the foregoing quotation. It was this same law that he had in mind when he wrote the following:

> Every violation of truth is not only a sort of suicide in the liar, but is a stab at the health of human society. On the most profitable lie the course of events presently lays a destructive tax; whilst frankness proves to be the best tactics, for it invites frankness, puts the parties on a convenient footing and makes their business a friendship. Trust men and they will be true to you; treat them greatly and they will show themselves great, though they make an exception in your favor to all their rules of trade.

◆

The Golden Rule philosophy is based upon a law which no man can circumvent. This law is the same law that is described in Lesson Eleven, on Accurate Thought, through the operation of which one's thoughts are transformed into reality corresponding exactly to the nature of the thoughts.

"Once grant the creative power of our thought and there is an end of struggling for our own way, and an end of gaining it *at some one else's expense;* for, since by the terms of the hypothesis we can create what we like, the simplest way of getting what we want is, not to snatch it from somebody else, but to make it for ourselves; and, since there is no limit to thought there can be no need for straining, and for everyone to have his own way in *this manner*, would be to banish all strife, want, sickness, and sorrow from the earth."

"Now, it is precisely on this assumption of the creative power of our thought that the whole Bible rests. If not, what is the meaning of being saved by Faith? Faith is essentially thought; and, therefore, every call to have faith in God is a call to trust in the power of our own thought about God. 'According to your faith be it unto you,' says the Old Testament. The entire book is nothing but one continuous statement of the creative power of Thought.

"The Law of Man's Individuality is, therefore, the Law of Liberty, and equally it is the Gospel of peace; for when we truly understand the law of our own individuality, we see that the same law finds its expression in everyone else; and, consequently, we shall reverence *the law in others* exactly in proportion as we value it in ourselves. To do this is to follow the Golden Rule of doing to others what we would they should do unto us; and because we know that the Law of Liberty in ourselves must include the free use of our creative power, there is no longer any inducement to infringe the rights of others, for we can satisfy all our desires by the exercise of our knowledge of the law.

"As this comes to be understood, co-operation will take the place of competition, with the result of removing all ground for enmity, whether between individuals, classes, or nations..."

(The foregoing quotation is from Bible Mystery and Bible Meaning by the late Judge T. Troward, published by Robert McBride & Company, New York City. Judge Troward was the author of several interesting volumes, among them The Edinburgh Lectures, which is recommended to all students of this course.)

If you wish to know what happens to a man when he totally disregards the law upon which the Golden Rule philosophy is based, pick out any man in your community whom you know to live for the single dominating purpose of accumulating wealth, and who has no conscientious scruples as to how he accumulates that wealth. Study this man and you will observe that there is no warmth to his soul; there is no kindness to his words; there is no welcome to his face. He has become a slave to the desire for wealth; he is too busy to enjoy life and too selfish to wish to help others enjoy it. He walks, and talks, and breathes, but he is nothing but a human automaton. Yet there are many who envy such a man and wish that they might occupy his position, foolishly believing him to be a *success.*

There can never be *success* without happiness, and no man can be happy without dispensing happiness to others. Moreover, the dispensation must be voluntary and with no other object in view than that of spreading sunshine into the hearts of those whose hearts are heavy-laden with burdens.

George D. Herron had in mind the law upon which the Golden Rule philosophy is based when he said:

"We have talked much of the brotherhood to come; but brotherhood has always been the fact of our life, long before it became a modern and inspired sentiment. Only we have been brothers in slavery and torment, brothers in ignorance and its perdition, brothers in disease, and war, and want, brothers in prostitution and hypocrisy. What happens to one of us sooner or later happens to all; we have always been unescapably involved in common destiny. The world constantly tends to the level of the down most man in it; and that down most man is the world's real ruler, hugging it close to his bosom, dragging it down to his death. You do not think so, but it is true, and it ought to be true. For if there were some way by which some of us could get free, apart from others, if there were some way by which some of us could have heaven while others had hell, if there were some way by which part of the world could escape some form of the blight and peril and misery of disinherited labor, then indeed would our world be lost and damned; but since men have never been able to separate themselves from one another's woes and wrongs, since history is fairly stricken with the lesson that we cannot escape brotherhood of some kind, since the whole of life is teaching us that we are hourly choosing between brotherhood in suffering and brotherhood in good, it remains for us to choose the brotherhood of a co-operative world, with all its fruits thereof—the fruits of *love* and *liberty.*

LEARN TO LIVE AND LET LIVE

The world war ushered us into an age of co-operative effort in which the law of "live and let live" stands out like a shining star to guide us in our relationships with each other. This great universal call for co-operative effort is taking on many forms, not the least important of which are the Rotary Clubs, the Kiwanis (dubs, the Lions Clubs and the many other luncheon clubs which bring men together in a spirit of friendly intercourse, for these clubs mark the beginning of an age of friendly competition in business. The next step will be a closer alliance of all such clubs in an out-and-out spirit of friendly cooperation.

The attempt by Woodrow Wilson and his contemporaries to establish the League of Nations, followed by the efforts of Warren G. Harding to give footing to the same cause under the name of the World Court, marked the first attempt in the history of the world to make the Golden Rule effective as a common meeting ground for the nations of the world.

There is no escape from the fact that the world has awakened to the truth in George D. Herron's statement that "we are hourly choosing between brotherhood in suffering and brotherhood in good." The world war has taught us—nay, forced upon us—the truth that a part of the world cannot suffer without injury to the whole world. These facts are called to your attention, not in the nature of a preachment on morality, but for the purpose of directing your attention to the underlying law through which these changes are being brought about. For more than four thousand years the world has been thinking about the Golden Rule philosophy, and that *thought* is now becoming transformed into realization of the benefits that accrue to those who apply it.

Still mindful of the fact that the student of this course is interested in a material success that can be measured by bank balances, it seems appropriate to suggest here that all who will may profit by shaping their business philosophy to conform with this sweeping change toward co-operation which is taking place all over the world.

If you can grasp the significance of the tremendous change that has come over the world since the close of the world war, and if you can interpret the meaning of all the luncheon clubs and other similar gatherings which bring men and women together in a spirit of friendly co-operation, surely your imagination will suggest to you the fact that this is an opportune time to profit by adopting this spirit of friendly co-operation as the basis of your own business or professional philosophy.

Stated conversely, it must be obvious to all who make any pretense of thinking accurately, that the time is at hand when failure to adopt the Golden Rule as the foundation of one's business or professional philosophy is the equivalent of economic suicide.

◆

Perhaps you have wondered why the subject of *honesty* has not been mentioned in this course, as a prerequisite to *success,* and, if so, the answer will be found in this lesson. The Golden Rule philosophy, when rightly understood and applied, makes dishonesty impossible. It does more than this—it makes impossible all the other destructive qualities such as selfishness, greed, envy, bigotry, hatred and malice.

When you apply the Golden Rule, you become, at one and the same time, both the judge and the judged—the accused and the accuser. This places one in a position in which *honesty* begins in one's own heart, toward one's self, and extends to all others with equal effect. *Honesty* based upon the Golden Rule is not the brand of honesty which recognizes nothing but the question of expediency.

It is no credit to be honest, when honesty is obviously the most *profitable* policy, lest one lose a good customer or a valuable client or be sent to jail for trickery. But when honesty means either a temporary or a permanent material loss, then it becomes an *honor* of the highest degree to all who practice it. Such honesty has its appropriate reward in the accumulated power of character and reputation enjoyed, by all who deserve it.

Those who understand and apply the Golden Rule philosophy are always scrupulously honest, not alone out of their desire to be just with others, but because: of their desire to be just with themselves. They understand the eternal law upon which the Golden Rule is based, and they know that through the operation of this law *every thought they release and every act in which they indulge has its counterpart in some fact or circumstance with which they will later be confronted.*

Golden Rule philosophers are honest because they understand the truth that honesty adds to their own character that "vital something" which gives it life and power. Those who understand the law through which the Golden Rule operates would poison their own drinking water as quickly as they would indulge in acts of injustice to others, for they know that such injustice starts a chain of causation that will not only bring them physical suffering, but will destroy their characters, stain for ill their reputations and render impossible the attainment of enduring success.

The law through which the Golden Rule philosophy operates is none other than the law through which the principle of Autosuggestion operates. This statement gives you a suggestion from which you should be able to make a deduction of a far-reaching nature and of inestimable value.

Test your progress in the mastery of this course by analyzing the foregoing statement and determining, before you read on, what suggestion it offers you.

Of what possible benefit could it be to you to know that when you do unto others as if you were the others, which is the sum and substance of the Golden Rule, you are putting into motion a chain of causation through the aid of a law which affects the others according to the nature of your act, *and at the same time planting in your character, through your subconscious mind, the effects of that act?*

This question practically suggests its own answer, but as

I am determined to cause you to think this vital subject out for yourself I will put the question in still another form, viz.:

If all your acts toward others, and even your thoughts of others, are registered in your subconscious mind, through the principle of Autosuggestion, thereby building your own character in exact duplicate of your *thoughts* and *acts,* can you not see how important it is to guard those acts and thoughts?

We are now in the very heart of the real reason for doing unto others as we would have them do unto us, for it is obvious that whatever we do unto others we do unto ourselves.

Stated in another way, every *act* and every *thought* you release modifies your own character in exact conformity with the nature of the act or thought, and your character is a sort of center of magnetic attraction which attracts to you the people and conditions that harmonize with it.

You cannot indulge in an act toward another person without having first created the nature of that act in your own *thought, and you cannot release a thought without planting the sum and substance and nature of it in your own sub-conscious mind, there to become a part and parcel of your own character.*

Grasp this simple principle and you will understand why you cannot afford to hate or envy another person. You will also understand why you cannot afford to strike back, in kind, at those who do you an injustice. Likewise, you will understand the injunction, "Return good for evil."

Understand the law upon which the Golden Rule injunction is based and you will understand, also, the law that eternally binds all mankind in a single bond of fellowship and renders it impossible for you to injure another person, by *thought or deed*, without injuring yourself; and, likewise, adds to your own character the results of every kind *thought* and *deed* in which you indulge.

Understand this law and you will then know, beyond room for the slightest doubt, that you are constantly punishing yourself for every wrong you commit and rewarding yourself for every act of constructive conduct in which you indulge.

It seems almost an act of Providence that the greatest wrong and the most severe injustice ever done me by one of my fellow men was done just as I began this lesson. (Some of the students of this course will know what it is to which I refer.)

This injustice has worked a temporary hardship on me, but that is of little consequence compared to the advantage it has given me by providing a timely opportunity for me to test the soundness of the entire premise upon which this lesson is founded.

The injustice to which I refer left two courses of action open to me. I could have claimed relief by "striking back" at my antagonist, through both civil court action and criminal libel proceedings, or I could have stood upon my right to forgive him. One course of action would have brought me a substantial sum—of money and whatever joy and satisfaction there may be in defeating and *punishing* an enemy. The other course of action would have brought me self-respect which is enjoyed by those who have successfully met the test and discovered that they have evolved to the point at which they can repeat the Lord's Prayer and *mean it!*

I chose the latter course. I did so, despite the recommendations of close personal friends to "strike back," and despite the offer of a prominent lawyer to do my "striking" for me *without cost.*

But the lawyer offered to do the impossible, for the reason that no man can "strike back" at another *without cost.* Not always is the cost of a monetary nature, for there are other things with which one may pay that are dearer than money.

It would be as hopeless to try to make one who was not

familiar with the law upon which the Golden Rule is based understand why I refused to strike back at this enemy as it would to try to describe the law of gravitation to an ape. If you understand this law you understand, also, why I chose to *forgive* my enemy.

In the Lord's Prayer we are admonished to forgive our enemies, but that admonition will fall on deaf ears except where the listener understands the law upon which it is based. That law is none other than the law upon which the Golden Rule is based. It is the law that forms the foundation of this entire lesson, and through which we must inevitably reap that which we sow. There is no escape from the operation of this law, nor is there any cause to try to avoid its consequences if we refrain from putting into motion *thoughts* and *acts* that are destructive.

That we may more concretely describe the law upon which this lesson is based, let us embody the law in a code of ethics such as one who wishes to follow literally the injunction of the Golden Rule might appropriately adopt, as follows.

MY CODE OF ETHICS

I. I believe in the Golden Rule as the basis of all human conduct; therefore, I will never do to another person that which I would not be willing for that person to do to me if our positions were reversed.

II. I will be honest, even to the slightest detail, in all my transactions with others, not alone because of my desire to be fair with them, but because of my desire to impress the idea of honesty on my own subconscious mind, thereby weaving this essential quality into my own character.

III. I will forgive those who are unjust toward me, with no

thought as to whether they deserve it or not, because I understand the law through which forgiveness of others strengthens my own character and wipes out the effects of my own transgressions, in my subconscious mind.

IV. I will be just, generous and fair with others always, even though I know that these acts will go unnoticed and unrecorded, in the ordinary terms of reward, because I understand and intend to apply the law through the aid of which one's own character is but the sum total of one's own *acts* and *deeds*.

V. Whatever time I may have to devote to the discovery and exposure of the weaknesses and faults of others I will devote, more profitably, to the discovery and *correction* of my own.

VI. I will slander no person, no matter how much I may believe another person may deserve it, because I wish to plant no destructive suggestions in my own subconscious mind.

VII. I recognize the power of Thought as being an inlet leading into my brain from the universal ocean of life; therefore, I will set no destructive thoughts afloat upon that ocean lest they pollute the minds of others.

VIII. I will conquer the common human tendency toward hatred, and envy, and selfishness, and jealousy, and malice, and pessimism, and doubt, and fear; for I believe these to be the seed from which the world harvests most of its troubles.

IX. When my mind is not occupied with thoughts that tend toward the attainment of my *definite chief aim* in life, I will voluntarily keep it filled with thoughts of courage, and self-confidence, and goodwill toward others, and faith, and kindness, and loyalty, and love for truth, and justice, for I believe these to be the seed from which the world reaps its harvest of progressive growth.

X. I understand that a mere passive belief in the soundness of the Golden Rule philosophy is of no value whatsoever, either to myself or to others; therefore, I will *actively* put into operation this universal rule for good in all my transactions with others.

XI. I understand the law through the operation of which my own character is developed from my own *acts* and *thoughts*; therefore, I will guard with care all that goes into its development.

XII. Realizing that enduring happiness comes only through helping others find it; that no act of kindness is without its reward, even though it may never be directly repaid, I will do my best to assist others when and where the opportunity appears.

You have noticed frequent reference to Emerson throughout this course. Every student of the course should own a copy of Emerson's Essays, and the essay on Compensation should be read and studied at least every three months. Observe, as you read this essay, that it deals with the same law as that upon which the Golden Rule is based.

There are people who believe that the Golden Rule philosophy is nothing more than a theory, and that it is in no way connected with an immutable law. They have arrived at this conclusion because of personal experience wherein they rendered service to others without enjoying the benefits of direct reciprocation.

How many are there who have not rendered service to others that was neither reciprocated nor appreciated? I am sure that I have had such an experience, not once, but many times, and I am equally sure that I will have similar experiences in the future, nor will I discontinue rendering service to others merely because *they* neither reciprocate nor appreciate my efforts.

And here is the reason:

When I render service to another, or indulge in an act of kindness, I store away in my sub-conscious mind the effect of my efforts, which may be likened to the "charging" of an electric battery. By and by, if I indulge in a sufficient number of such acts I will have developed a positive, dynamic character that will *attract* to me people who harmonize with or resemble my own character.

Those whom I *attract* to me will reciprocate the acts of kindness and the service that I have rendered others, thus the Law of Compensation will have balanced the scales of justice for me, bringing back from one source the results of service that I rendered through an entirely different source.

You have often heard it said that a salesman's first sale should be to himself, which means that unless he first convinces himself of the merits of his wares he will not be able to convince others. Here, again, enters this same Law of Attraction, for it is a well-known fact that *enthusiasm* is contagious, and when a salesman shows great *enthusiasm* over his wares he will arouse a corresponding interest in the minds of others.

You can comprehend this law quite easily by regarding yourself as a sort of human magnet that attracts those whose characters harmonize with your own. In thus regarding yourself as a magnet that attracts to you all who harmonize with your dominating characteristics and repels all who do not so harmonize, you should keep in mind, also, the fact that *you are the builder of that magnet;* also, that you may change its nature so that it will correspond to any ideal that you may wish to set up and follow.

And, most important of all, you should keep in mind the fact that this entire process of change takes place through *thought!*

Your character is but the sum total of your *thoughts* and *deeds!* This truth has been stated in many different ways throughout this course.

Because of this great truth it is impossible for you to render any useful service or indulge in any act of kindness toward others without benefiting thereby. Moreover, it is just as impossible for you to indulge in any destructive *act* or *thought* without paying the penalty in the loss of a corresponding amount of your own power.

◆

Positive thought develops a dynamic personality. *Negative thought* develops a personality of an opposite nature. In many of the preceding lessons of this course, and in this one, definite instructions are given as to the exact method of developing personality through *positive thought.* All of the formulas provided in this course are for the purpose of helping you *consciously* to direct the power of *thought* in the development of a personality that will attract to you those who will be of help in the attainment of your *definite chief aim.*

You need no proof that your hostile or unkind *acts* toward others bring back the effects of retaliation. Moreover, this retaliation is usually definite and immediate. Likewise, you need no proof that you can accomplish more by dealing with others in such a way that they will want to co-operate with you. If you master the lesson on Self-control, you will understand how to induce others to act toward you as you wish them to act—*through your own attitude toward them.*

The law of "an eye for an eye and a tooth for a tooth" is

based upon the selfsame law as that upon which the Golden Rule operates. This is nothing more than the law of retaliation with which all of us are familiar. Even the most selfish person will respond to this law, *because he cannot help it!* If I speak ill of you, even though I tell the truth, you will not think kindly of me. Furthermore, you will most likely retaliate in kind. But, if I speak of your virtues you will think kindly of me, and when the opportunity appears you will reciprocate in kind in the majority of instances.

Through the operation of this law of attraction the uninformed are constantly attracting trouble and grief and hatred and opposition from others by their *unguarded words* and *destructive acts.*

Do unto others as you would have them do unto you!

We have heard that injunction expressed thousands of times, yet how many of us understand the law upon which it is based? To make this injunction somewhat clearer it might be well to state it more in detail, about as follows:

Do unto others as you would have them do unto you, *bearing in mind the fact that human nature has a tendency to retaliate in kind.*

Confucius must have had in mind the law of retaliation when he stated the Golden Rule philosophy in about this way:

Do not unto others that which you would not have them do unto you.

And he might well have added an explanation to the effect that the reason for his injunction was based upon the common tendency of man to retaliate in kind.

Those who do not understand the law upon which the Golden Rule is based are inclined to argue that it will not work, for the reason that men are inclined toward the principle of exacting "an eye for an eye and a tooth for a tooth," which is nothing more nor less than the law of retaliation. If they would go a step further in their reasoning they would understand that they are looking at the *negative* effects of this law, and that the selfsame law is capable of producing *positive* effects as well.

In other words, if you would not have your own eye plucked out, then insure against this misfortune by refraining from plucking out the other fellow's eye. Go a step further and render the other fellow an act of kindly, helpful service, and *through the operation of this same law of retaliation* he will render you a similar service.

And, if he should fail to reciprocate your kindness—what then?

You have profited, nevertheless, because of the effect of your act on *your own subconscious mind!*

Thus by indulging in acts of kindness and applying, always, the Golden Rule philosophy, you are sure of benefit from one source and at the same time you have a pretty fair chance of profiting from another source.

It might happen that you would base all of your acts toward others on the Golden Rule without enjoying any direct reciprocation for a long period of time, and it might so happen that those to whom you rendered those acts of kindness would never reciprocate, but meantime you have been adding vitality to your own character and sooner or later this *positive character* which you have been building will begin to assert itself and you will discover that you have been receiving compound interest on compound interest in return for those acts of kindness which appeared to have been wasted on those who neither appreciated nor reciprocated them.

Remember that your *reputation* is made by others, but your *character* is made by *you!*

You want your reputation to be a favorable one, but you cannot be sure that it will be for the reason that it is something that exists outside of your own control, in the minds of others. It is what others believe you to be. With your character it is different. Your character is that which *you are,* as the results of your *thoughts* and *deeds.* You control it. You can make it weak, good or bad. When you are satisfied and know in your mind that your character is above reproach you need not worry about your reputation, for it is as impossible for your character to be destroyed or damaged by anyone except yourself as it is to destroy matter or energy.

It was this truth that Emerson had in mind when he said: "A political victory, a rise of rents, the recovery of your sick or the return of your absent friend, or some other quite external event raises your spirits, and you think your days are prepared for you. *Do not believe it.* It can never be so. *Nothing can bring you peace but yourself. Nothing can bring you peace but the triumph of principles.*"

One reason for being just toward others is the fact that such action may cause them to reciprocate, in kind, but a better reason is the fact that kindness and justice toward others develop *positive character* in all who indulge in these acts.

You may withhold from me the reward to which I am entitled for rendering you helpful service, but no one can deprive me of the benefit I will derive from the rendering of that service in so far as it adds to my own *character.*

GOLDEN RULE PHILOSOPHY

We are living in a great industrial age. Everywhere we see the evolutionary forces working great changes in the method and manner of living, and re-arranging the relationships between men, in the ordinary pursuit of life, liberty and a living.

This is an age of organized effort. On every hand we see evidence that organization is the basis of all financial success, and while other factors than that of organization enter into the attainment of success, this factor is still one of major importance.

This industrial age has created two comparatively new terms. One is called "capital" and the other "labor." Capital and labor constitute the main wheels in the machinery of organized effort. These two great forces enjoy success in exact ratio to the extent that both understand and apply the Golden Rule philosophy. Despite this fact, however, harmony between these two forces does not always prevail, thanks to the destroyers of confidence who make a living by sowing the seed of dissension and stirring up strife between employers and employees.

During the past fifteen years I have devoted considerable time to the study of the causes of disagreement between employers and employees. Also, I have gathered much information on this subject from other men who, likewise, have been studying this problem.

There is but one solution which will, if understood by all concerned, bring harmony out of chaos and establish a perfect working relationship between capital and labor. The remedy is no invention of mine. It is based upon a great universal law of Nature. This remedy bas been well stated by one of the great men of this generation, in the following words:

"The question we propose to consider is exciting deep interest at the present time, but no more than its importance demands. It is one of the hopeful signs of the times that these subjects of vital interest to human happiness are constantly coming up for a bearing, are engaging the attention of the wisest men, and stirring the minds of all classes of people. The wide prevalence of this movement shows that a new life is beating in the heart of humanity, operating upon their faculties like the warm breath of spring upon the frozen ground and the dormant germs of the plant. It will make a great stir, it will break up many frozen and dead forms, it will produce great and, in some cases, it may be, destructive changes, but it announces the blossoming of new hopes, and the coming of new harvests for the supply of human wants and the means of greater happiness. There is great need of wisdom to guide the new forces coming into action. Every man is under the most solemn obligation to do his part in forming a correct public opinion and giving wise direction to popular will.

"The only solution for the problems of labor, of want, of abundance, of suffering and sorrow can only be found by regarding them from a moral and spiritual point of view. They must be seen end examined in a light that is not of themselves. *The true relations of labor and capital can never be discovered by human selfishness.* They must be viewed from a higher purpose than wages or the accumulation of wealth. They must be regarded from their bearing upon the purposes for which men was created. It is from this point of view I propose to consider the subject before us.

"Capital and labor are essential to each other. Their interests are so bound together that they cannot be separated. In civilized and enlightened communities they are mutually dependent. If there is any difference, capital is more dependent upon labor than labor upon capital. Life can be sustained without capital. Animals, with a few exceptions, have no property, and take no anxious thought for the morrow, and our Lord commends them to our notice as examples worthy of imitation. 'Behold the fowls of the air,' He says, 'for they sow not, neither do they reap nor gather into barns, yet your heavenly Father feedeth them.' The savages live without capital. Indeed, the great mass of human beings live by their labor from day to day, from hand to mouth. But no man can live upon his wealth. He cannot eat his gold and silver; he cannot clothe himself with deeds and certificates of stock. Capital can do nothing without labor, *and its only value consists in its power to purchase labor or its results.* It is itself the product of labor. It has no occasion, therefore, to assume an importance that does not belong to it. Absolutely dependent, however, as it is upon labor for its value, it is an essential factor in human progress.

"The moment man begins to rise from a savage and comparatively independent state to a civilized and dependent one, capital becomes necessary. Men come into more intimate relations with one another. Instead of each one doing everything, men begin to devote themselves to special employments, and to depend upon others to provide many things for them while they engage in some special occupation. In this way labor becomes diversified. One man works in iron, another in wood; one manufactures cloth, another makes it into garments; some raise food to feed those who build houses and manufacture implements of husbandry. This necessitates a system of exchanges, and to facilitate exchanges roads must be made, and men must be employed to make them. As population increases and necessities multiply, the business of exchange becomes enlarged, until we have immense manufactories, railroads girding the earth with iron bends, steamships plowing every sea, and a multitude of men who cannot raise bread or make a garment, or do anything directly for the supply of their own wants.

"Now, we can see how we become more dependent upon others as our wants are multiplied and civilization advances. Each one works in his special employment, does better work, because he can devote his whole thought and time to a form of use for which he is specially fitted, and contributes more largely to the public good. While he is working for others, all others are working for him. Every member of the community is working for the whole body, and the whole body for every member. This is the law of perfect life, a law which rules everywhere in the material body. Every man who is engaged in any employment useful to body or mind is a philanthropist, a public benefactor, whether he raises corn on the prairie, cotton in Texas or India, mines coal in the chambers of the earth, or feeds it to engines in the hold of a steamship. If selfishness did not pervert and blast human motives, all men and women would be fulfilling the law of charity while engaged in their daily employment.

"To carry on this vast system of exchanges, to place the forest and the farm, the factory and the mine side by side, and deliver the products of all climes at every door, requires immense capital. One man cannot work his farm or factory, and build a railroad or a line of steamships. As raindrops acting singly cannot drive a mill or supply steam for an engine, but, collected in a vast reservoir, become the resistless power of Niagara, or the force which drives the engine and steamship like mighty shuttles from mountain to seacoast and from shore to shore, so a few dollars in a multitude of pockets are powerless to provide the means for these vast operations, but combined they move the world.

"Capital is a friend of labor and essential to its economical exercise and just reward. It can be, and often is, a terrible enemy, when employed for selfish purposes alone; but the great mass of it is more friendly to human happiness than is generally supposed. It cannot be employed without in some way, either directly or indirectly, helping the laborer. We think of the evils we suffer, but allow the good we enjoy to pass unnoticed. We think of the evils that larger means would relieve and the comforts they would provide, but overlook the blessings we enjoy that would have been impossible without large accumulations of capital. It is the part of wisdom to form a just estimate of the good we receive as well as the evils we suffer.

"It is a common saying at the present time, that the rich are growing richer and the poor poorer; but when all man's possessions are taken into the account there are good reasons for doubting this assertion. It is true that the rich are growing richer. It is also true that the condition of the laborer is constantly improving. *The common laborer has conveniences and comforts which princes could not command a century ago.* He is better clothed, has a greater variety and abundance of food, lives in a more comfortable dwelling, and has many more conveniences for the conduct of domestic affairs and the prosecution of labor than money could purchase but a few years ago. An emperor could not travel with the ease, the comfort, and the swiftness that the common laborer can today. He may think that he stands alone, with no one to help. But, in truth, he has an immense retinue of servants constantly waiting upon him, ready and anxious to do his bidding. It requires a vast army of men and an immense outlay of capital to provide a common dinner, such as every man and woman, with few exceptions, has enjoyed today.

"Think of the vast combination of means and men and forces necessary to provide even a frugal meal. The Chinaman raises your tea, the Brazilian your coffee, the East Indian your spices, the Cuban your sugar, the farmer upon the western prairies your bread and possibly your beef, the gardener your vegetables, the dairyman your butter and milk; the miner has dug from the hills the coal with which your food was cooked and your house was warmed, the cabinet-maker has provided you with chairs and tables, the cutler with knives and forks, the potter with dishes, the Irishman has made your tablecloth, the butcher has dressed your meat, the miller your flour.

"But these various articles of food, and the means of preparing and serving them, were produced at immense distances from you and from one another. Oceans had to be traversed, hills leveled, valleys filled, and mountains tunneled, ships must be built, railways constructed, and a vast army of men instructed and employed in every mechanical art before the materials for your dinner could be prepared and served. There must also be men to collect these materials, to buy and sell and distribute them. Everyone stands in his own place and does his own work, and receives his wages. But he is none the less working for you, and serving you as truly and effectively as he would be if he were in your special employment and received his wages from your hand. In the light of these facts, which everyone must acknowledge, we may be able to see more clearly the truth, that every man and woman who does useful work is a public benefactor, and the thought of it and the purpose of it will ennoble the labor and the laborer. We are all bound together by common ties. The rich and the poor, the learned and the ignorant, the strong and the weak, are woven together in one social and civic web. Harm to one is harm to all; help to one is help to all.

"You see what a vast army of servants it requires to provide your dinner. Do you not see that it demands a corresponding amount of capital to provide and keep this complicated machinery in motion? And do you not see that every man, woman and child is enjoying the benefit of it? How could we get our coal, our meat, our flour, our tea and coffee, sugar and rice? The laborer cannot build ships and sail them and support himself while doing it. *The farmer cannot leave his farm and take his produce to the market. The miner cannot mine and transport his coal.* The farmer in Kansas may be burning corn today to cook his food and warm his dwelling, and the miner may be hungry for the bread which the corn would supply, because they cannot exchange the fruits of their labor. Every acre of land, every forest and mine has been increased in value by railways and steamboats, and the comforts of life and the means of social and intellectual culture have been carried to the most inaccessible places.

"But the benefits of capital are not limited to supplying present wants and comforts. It opens new avenues for labor. It diversifies it and gives a wider field to everyone to do the kind of work for which he is best fitted by natural taste and genius. The number of employments created by railways, steamships, telegraph, and manufactories by machinery can hardly be estimated. Capital is also largely invested in supplying the means of intellectual and spiritual culture. Books are multiplied at constantly diminishing prices, and the best thought of the world, by means of our great publishing houses, is made accessible to the humblest workman. There is no better example of the benefits the common laborer derives from capital than the daily newspaper. For two or three cents the history of the world for twenty-four hours is brought to every door. The laborer, while riding to or from his work in a comfortable car, can visit all parts of the known world and get a truer idea of the events of the day than he could if he were bodily present. A battle in China or Africa, an earthquake in Spain, a dynamite explosion in London, a debate in Congress, the movements of men in public and private life for the suppression of vice, for enlightening the ignorant, helping the needy, and improving the people generally, are spread before him in a small compass, and bring him into contact and on equality, in regard to the world's history, with kings and queens, with saints and sages, and people in every condition in life. *Do you ever think,* while reading the morning paper, how many men have been running on your errands, collecting intelligence for you from all parts of the earth, and putting it into a form convenient for your use? It required the investment of millions of money and the employment of thousands of men to produce that paper and leave it at your door. And what did all this service cost you? A few cents.

"These are examples of the benefits which everyone derives from capital, benefits which could not be obtained without vast expenditures of money; benefits which come to us without our care and lay their blessings at our feet. Capital cannot be invested in any useful production without blessing a multitude of people. It sets the machinery of life in motion, it multiplies employment; it places the product of all climes at every door, it draws the people of all nations together; brings mind in contact with mind, and gives to every man and woman a large and valuable share of the product. These are facts which it would be well for everyone, however poor he may be, to consider.

"If capital is such a blessing to labor; if it can only be brought into use by labor, and derives all its value from it, how can there be any conflict between them? There could be none if both the capitalist and laborer acted from humane and Christian principles. But they do not. They are governed by inhuman and unchristian principles. Each party seeks to get the largest returns for the least service. Capital desires larger profits, labor higher wages. The interests of the capitalist and the laborer come into direct collision. In this warfare capital has great advantages, and has been prompt to take them. It has demanded and taken the lion's share of the profits. It has despised the servant that enriched it. It has regarded the laborer as a menial, a slave, whose rights and happiness it was not bound to respect. It influences legislators to enact laws in its favor, subsidizes governments and wields its power for its own advantage. Capital has been a lord and labor a servant. While the servant remained docile and obedient, content with such compensation as its lord chose to give, there was no conflict. But labor is rising from a servile, submissive, and hopeless condition. It has acquired strength and intelligence; has gained the idea that it has rights that has rights that ought to be respected, and begins to assert and combine to support them.

"Each party in this warfare regards the subject from its own selfish interests. The capitalist supposes that gain to labor is loss to him, and that he must look to his own interests first; that the cheaper the labor the larger his gains. Consequently it is for his interest to keep the price as low as possible. On the contrary, the laborer thinks that he loses what the capitalist gains, and, consequently, that it is for his interest to get as large wages as possible. From these opposite points of view their interests appear to be directly hostile. What one party gains the other loses; hence the conflict. Both are acting from selfish motives, and, consequently, must be wrong. Both parties see only half of the truth, and, mistaking that for the whole of it, they fall into a mistake ruinous to both. Each one stands on his own ground, and regards the subject wholly from his point of view and in the misleading light of his own selfishness. Passion inflames the mind and blinds the understanding; and when passion is aroused men will sacrifice their own interests to injure others, and both will suffer loss. They will wage continual warfare against each other; they will resort to all devices, and take advantage of every necessity to win a victory. Capital tries to starve the laborer into submission, like a beleaguered city; and hunger and want are most powerful weapons. Labor sullenly resists, and tries to destroy the value of capital by rendering it unproductive. If necessity or interest compels a truce, it is a sullen one, and maintained with the purpose of renewing hostilities as soon as there is any prospect of success. Thus laborers and capitalists confront each other like two armed hosts, ready at any time to renew the conflict. *It will be renewed, without doubt, and continued with varying success until both parties discover that they are mistaken, that their interests are mutual, and can only be secured to the fullest extent by co-operation and giving to each the reward it deserves.* The capitalist and the laborer must clasp hands across the bottomless pit into which so much wealth and work has been cast.

"How this reconciliation is to be effected is a question that is occupying the minds of many wise and good men on both sides at the present time. Wise and impartial legislation will, no doubt, be an important agent in restraining blind passion and protecting all classes from insatiable greed; and it is the duty of every man to use his best endeavors to secure such legislation both in state and national governments. Organizations of laborers for protecting their own rights and securing a better reward for their labor, will have a great influence. That influence will continue to increase as their temper becomes normal and firm, and their demands are based *on justice and humanity.* Violence and threats will effect no good. Dynamite, whether in the form of explosives or the more destructive force of fierce and reckless passion, will heal no wounds nor subdue any hostile feeling. Arbitration is, doubtless, the wisest and most practicable means now available to bring about amicable relations between these hostile parties and secure justice to both. Giving the laborer a share in the profits of the business has worked well in some cases, but it is attended with great practical difficulties which require more wisdom, self-control and genuine regard for the common interests of both parties than often can be found. Many devices may have a partial and temporary effect. But no permanent progress can be made in settling this conflict without restraining and finally removing its cause.

"Its real central cause is an inordinate love of self and the world, and that cause will continue to operate as long as it exists. It may be restrained and moderated, but it will assert itself when occasion offers. Every wise man must, therefore, seek to remove the cause, and as far as he can do it he will control effects. Purify the fountain, and you make the whole stream pure and wholesome.

"There is a principle of universal influence that must underlie and guide every successful effort to bring these two great factors of human good which now confront each other with hostile purpose, into harmony. It is no invention or discovery of mine. It embodies a higher than human wisdom. It is not difficult to understand or apply. The child can comprehend it and act according to it. It is universal in its application, and wholly useful in its effects. It will lighten the burdens of labor and increase its rewards. It will give security to capital and make it more productive. It is simply the Golden Rule, embodied in these words: *'Therefore all things whatsoever ye would that men should do to you, do ye even so to them: for this is the law and the prophets.'*

"Before proceeding to apply this principle to the case in hand, let me call your special attention to it. It is a very remarkable law of human life which seems to have been generally overlooked by statesmen, philosophers and religious teachers. This rule embodies the whole of religion; it comprises all the precepts, commandments, and means of the future triumphs of good over evil, of truth over error, and the peace and happiness of men, foretold in the glorious visions of the prophets. Mark the words. It does not merely say that it is a wise rule; that it accords with the principles of the Divine order revealed in the law and the prophets. *It embodies them all; it 'IS the law and the prophets.'* It comprises love to God. It says we should regard Him as we desire to have Him regard us; that we should do to Him as we wish to have Him do to us. If we desire to have Him love us with all His heart, with all His soul, with all His mind, and with all His strength, we must love Him in the same manner. If we desire to have our neighbor love us as he loves himself, we must love him as we love ourself. Here, then, is the universal and Divine law of human service and fellowship. It is not a precept of human wisdom; it has its origin in the Divine nature, and its embodiment in human nature. Now, let us apply it to the conflict between labor and capital.

"You are a capitalist. Your money is invested in manufactures, in land, in mines, in merchandise, railways, and ships, or you loan it to others on interest. You employ, directly or indirectly, men to use your capital. You cannot come to a just conclusion concerning your rights and duties and privileges by looking wholly at your own gains. The glitter of the silver and gold will exercise so potent a spell over your mind that it will blind you to everything else. You can see no interest but your own. The laborer is not known or regarded as a man who has any interests you are bound to regard. You see him only as your slave, your tool, your means of adding to your wealth. In this light he is a friend so far as he serves you, an enemy so far as he does not. But change your point of view. Put yourself in his place; put him in your place. How would you like to have him treat you if you were in his place? Perhaps you have been there. In all probability you have, for the capitalist today was the laborer yesterday, and the laborer today will be the employer tomorrow. You know from lively and painful experience how you would like to be treated. Would you like to be regarded as a mere tool? As a means of enriching another? Would you like to have your wages kept down to the bare necessities of life? Would you like to be regarded with indifference and treated with brutality? Would you like to have your blood, your strength, your soul coined into dollars for the benefit of another? These questions are easy to answer. Everyone knows that he would rejoice to be treated kindly, to have his interests regarded, his rights recognized and protected. Everyone knows that such regard awakens a response in his own heart. Kindness begets kindness; respect awakens respect. Put yourself in his place. Imagine that you are dealing with yourself, and you will have no difficulty in deciding whether you should give the screw another turn, that you may wring a penny more from the muscles of the worker, or relax its pressure, and, if possible, add something to his wages, and give him respect for his service. Do to him as you would have him do to you in changed conditions.

"You are a laborer. You receive a certain sum for a day's work. Put yourself in the place of your employer. How would you like to have the men you employed work for you? Would you think it right that they should regard you as their enemy? Would you think it honest in them to slight their work, *to do as little and to get as much as possible?* If you had a large contract which must be completed at a fixed time or you would suffer great loss, would you like to have your workmen take advantage of your necessity to compel an increase of their wages? Would you think it right and wise in them to interfere with you in the management of your business? To dictate whom you should employ, and on what terms you should employ them? Would you not rather have them do honest work in a kind and good spirit? Would you not be much more disposed to look to their interests, to lighten their labor, to increase their wages when you could afford to do so, and look after the welfare of their families, when you found that they regarded yours? I know that it would be so. It is true that men are selfish, and that some men are so mean and contracted in spirit that they cannot see any interest but their own; whose hearts, not made of flesh but of silver and gold, are so hard that they are not touched by any human feeling, and care not how much others suffer if they can make a cent by it. But they are the exception, not the rule. We are influenced by the regard and devotion of others to our interests. The laborer who knows that his employer feels kindly toward him, desires to treat him justly and to regard his good, will do better work and more of it, and will be disposed to look to his employer's interests as well as his own.

"I am well aware that many will think this Divine and humane law of doing to others as we would have them do to us, is impracticable in this selfish and worldly age. If both parties would be governed by it, everyone can see how happy would be the results. But, it will be said, they will not. The laborer will not work unless compelled by want. He will take advantage of every necessity. As soon as he gains a little independence of his employer he becomes proud, arrogant and hostile. The employer will seize upon every means to keep the workmen dependent upon him, and to make as much out of them as possible. Every inch of ground which labor yields capital will occupy and intrench itself in it, and from its vantage bring the laborer into greater dependence and more abject submission. But this is a mistake. The history of the world testifies that when the minds of men are not embittered by intense hostility and their feelings outraged by cruel wrongs, they are ready to listen to calm, disinterested and judicious counsel. A man who employed a large number of laborers in mining coal told me that he had never known an instance to fail of a calm and candid response when he had appealed to honorable motives, as a man to man, both of whom acknowledged a common humanity. There is a recent and most notable instance in this city of the happy effect of calm, disinterested and judicious counsel in settling difficulties between employers and workmen that were disastrous to both.

"When the mind is inflamed by passion men will not listen to reason. They become blind to their own interests and regardless of the interests of others. *Difficulties are never settled while passion rages. They are never settled by conflict. One party may be subdued by power; but the sense of wrong will remain; the fire of passion will slumber ready to break out again on the first occasion.* But let the laborer or the capitalist feel assured that the other party has no wish to take any advantage, that there is a sincere desire and determination on both sides to be just and pay due regard to their common interests, and all the conflict between them would cease, as the wild waves of the ocean sink to calm when the winds are at rest. The laborer and the capitalist have a mutual and common interest. Neither can permanently prosper without the prosperity of the other. They are parts of one body. If labor is the arm, capital is the blood. Devitalize or waste the blood, and the arm loses its power. Destroy the arm, and the blood is useless. Let each care for the other, and both are benefited. *Let each take the Golden Rule as a guide,* and all cause of hostility will be removed, all conflict will cease, and they will go hand in hand to do their work and reap their just reward."

POINTS TO REMEMBER

1. The Golden Rule means to do unto others as you would wish them to do unto you.
2. What you sow, you shall reap.
3. No man can attain success in its highest form without the aid of earnest prayer!

4

ENTHUSIASM

Enthusiasm is a state of mind that inspires and arouses one to put *action* into the task at hand. It does more than this—it is contagious, and vitally affects not only the enthusiast, but all with whom he comes in contact.

Enthusiasm bears the same relationship to a human being that steam does to the locomotive—it is the vital moving force that impels *action.* The greatest leaders of men are those who know how to inspire enthusiasm in their followers. Enthusiasm is the most important factor entering into salesmanship. It is, by far, the most vital factor that enters into public speaking.

If you wish to understand the difference between a man who is enthusiastic and one who is not, compare Billy Sunday with the average man of his profession. The finest sermon ever delivered would fall upon deaf ears if it were not backed with enthusiasm by the speaker.

HOW ENTHUSIASM WILL AFFECT YOU

Mix enthusiasm with your work and it will not seem hard or monotonous. Enthusiasm will so energize your entire body that you can get along with less than half the usual amount of sleep and at the same time it will enable you to perform from two to three times as much work as you usually perform in a given period, without fatigue.

For many years I have done most of my writing at night. One night, while I was enthusiastically at work over my typewriter, I looked out of the window of my study, just across the square from the Metropolitan tower, in New York City, and saw what seemed to be the most peculiar reflection of the moon on the tower. It was of a silvery gray shade, such as I had never seen before. Upon closer inspection I found that the reflection was that of the early morning sun and not that of the moon. It was daylight! I had been at work all night, but I was so engrossed in my work that the night had passed as though it were but an hour. I worked at my task all that day and all the following night without stopping, except for a small amount of light food.

Two nights and one day without sleep, and with but little food, without the slightest evidence of fatigue, would not have been possible had I not kept my body energized with *enthusiasm* over the work at hand.

Enthusiasm is not merely a figure of speech; it is a vital force that you can harness and use with profit. Without it you would resemble an electric battery without electricity.

Enthusiasm is the vital force with which you recharge your body and develop a dynamic personality. Some people are blessed with natural *enthusiasm*, while others must acquire it. The procedure through which it may be developed is simple. It begins by the doing of the work or rendering of the service which one likes best. If you should be so situated that you cannot conveniently engage in the work which you like best, for the time being, then you can proceed along another line very effectively by adopting a *definite chief aim* that contemplates your engaging in that particular work at some future time.

Lack of capital and many other circumstances over which you have no immediate control may force you to engage in work which you do not like, but no one can stop you from determining in your own mind what your *definite chief aim* in life shall be, nor can anyone stop you from planning ways and means for translating this aim into reality, nor can anyone stop you from mixing *enthusiasm* with your plans.

Happiness, the final object of all human effort, is a state of mind that can be maintained only through the hope of future achievement. Happiness lies always in the future and never in the past. The happy person is the one who dreams of heights of achievement that are yet unattained. The home you intend to own, the money you intend to earn and place in the bank, the trip you intend to take when you can afford it, the Position in life you intend to fill when you have prepared yourself, and the preparation, itself—these are the things that produce happiness. Likewise, these are the materials out of which your *definite chief aim* is formed; these are the things over which you may become *enthusiastic*, no matter what your present station in life may be.

More than twenty years ago I became enthusiastic over an idea. When the idea first took form in my mind I was unprepared to take even the first step toward its transformation into reality. But I nursed it in my mind—I became *enthusiastic* over it as I looked ahead, in my imagination, and saw the time when I would be prepared to make it a reality.

The idea was this: I wanted to become the editor of a magazine, based upon the Golden Rule, through which I could inspire people to keep up courage and deal with one another squarely.

Finally my chance came! and, on armistice day, 1918, I wrote the first editorial for what was to become the material realization of a hope that had lain dormant in my mind for nearly a score of years.

With *enthusiasm* I poured into that editorial the emotions which I had been developing in my heart over a period of more than twenty years. My dream had come true. My editorship of a national magazine had become a reality.

As I have stated, this editorial was written with *enthusiasm.* I took it to a man of my acquaintance and with *enthusiasm* I read it to him. The editorial ended in these words: "At last my twenty-year-old dream is about to come true. It takes money, and a lot of it, to publish a national magazine, and I haven't the slightest idea where I am going to get this essential factor, but this is worrying me not at all because *I know I am going to get it somewhere!"* As I wrote those lines, I mixed *enthusiasm* and faith with them.

I had hardly finished reading this editorial when the man to whom I read it—the first and only person to whom I had shown it—said:

"I can tell you where you are going to get the money, for I am going to supply it." And he did!

Yes, *enthusiasm* is a vital force; so vital, in fact, that no man who has it highly developed can begin even to approximate his power of achievement.

Before passing to the next step in this lesson, I wish to repeat and to emphasize the fact that you may develop *enthusiasm* over your *definite chief aim* in life, no matter whether you are in position to achieve that purpose at this time or not. You may be a long way from realization of your *definite chief aim,* but if you will kindle the fire of *enthusiasm* in your heart, and keep it burning, before very long the obstacles that now stand in the way of your attainment of that purpose will melt away as if by the force of magic, and you will find yourself in possession of power that you did not know you possessed.

HOW YOUR ENTHUSIASM WILL AFFECT OTHERS

We come, now, to the discussion of one of the most important subjects of this Reading Course, namely, *suggestion.*

In the preceding lessons we have discussed the subject of *Autosuggestion,* which is self-suggestion.

Suggestion is the principle through which your words and your acts and even *your state of mind* influence others. That you may comprehend the far-reaching power of *suggestion,* let me refer to the Introductory Lesson, in which the principle of telepathy is described. If you now understand and accept the principle of telepathy (the communication of thought from one mind to another without the aid of signs, symbols or sounds) as a reality, you of course understand why *enthusiasm* is contagious, and why it influences all within its radius.

When your own mind is vibrating at a high rate, because it has been stimulated with *enthusiasm,* that vibration registers in the minds of all within its radius, and especially in the minds of those with whom you come in close contact. When a public speaker "senses" the feeling that his audience is "en rapport" with him he merely recognizes the fact that his own *enthusiasm* has influenced the minds of his listeners until their minds are vibrating in harmony with his own.

When the salesman "senses" the fact that the "psychological" moment for closing a sale has arrived, he merely feels the effect of his own *enthusiasm* as it influences the mind of his prospective buyer and places that mind "en rapport" (in harmony) with his own.

The subject of *suggestion* constitutes so vitally an important part of this lesson, and of this entire course, that I will now proceed to describe the three mediums through which it usually operates; namely, what you say, what you do and what you *think!*

When you are enthusiastic over the goods you are selling or the services you are offering, or the speech you are delivering, your state of mind becomes obvious to all who hear you, *by the tone of your voice.*

Whether you have ever thought of it in this way or not, it is the tone in which you make a statement, more than it is the statement itself, that carries conviction or fails to convince. No mere combination of words can ever take the place of a deep belief in a statement that is expressed with burning *enthusiasm.* Words are but devitalized sounds unless colored with feeling that is born of *enthusiasm.*

Here the printed word fails me, for I can never express with mere type and paper the difference between words that fall from unemotional lips, without the fire of *enthusiasm* hack of them, and those which seem to pour forth from a heart that is bursting with eagerness for expression. The difference is there, however.

Thus, *what you say,* and the way in which you say it, conveys a meaning that may be just the opposite to what is intended. This accounts for many a failure by the salesman who presents his arguments in words which seem logical enough, but lack the coloring that can come only from *enthusiasm* that is born of sincerity and belief in the goods he is trying to sell. His words said one thing, but the tone of his voice *suggested* something entirely different; therefore, no sale was made.

That which you *say* is an important factor in the operation of the principle of *suggestion,* but not nearly so important as that which you *do. Your acts will count for more than your words,* and woe unto you if the two fail to harmonize.

If a man preach the Golden Rule as a sound rule of conduct his words will fall upon deaf ears if he does not practice that which he preaches. The most effective sermon that any man can preach on the soundness of the Golden Rule is that which he preaches, by *suggestion,* when he applies this rule in his relationships with his fellow men.

If a salesman of Ford automobiles drives up to his prospective purchaser in a Buick, or some other make of car, all the arguments he can present in behalf of the Ford will be without effect. Once I went into one of the offices of the Dictaphone Company to look at a Dictaphone (dictating machine). The salesman in charge presented a logical argument as to the machine's merits, while the stenographer at his side was transcribing letters from a shorthand notebook. His arguments in favor of a dictating machine, as compared with the old method of dictating to a stenographer, did not impress me, because his actions were not in harmony with his words.

Your *thoughts* constitute the most important of the three ways in which you apply the principle of *suggestion,* for the reason that they control the tone of your words and, to some extent at least, your actions. If your *thoughts* and your *actions* and your *words* harmonize, you are bound to influence those with whom you come in contact, more or less toward your way of thinking.

We will now proceed to analyze the subject of *suggestion* and to show you exactly how to apply the principle upon which it operates. As we have already seen, *suggestion* differs from Autosuggestion only in one way—we use it, consciously or unconsciously, when we influence others, while we use *Autosuggestion* as a means of influencing ourselves.

Before you can influence another person through *suggestion,* that person's mind must be in a state of neutrality; that is, it must be open and receptive to your method of *suggestion.* Right here is where most salesmen fail—they try to make a sale before the mind of the prospective buyer has been rendered receptive or neutralized. This is such a vital point in this lesson that I feel impelled to dwell upon it until there can be no doubt that you understand the principle that I am describing.

When I say that the salesman must neutralize the mind of his prospective purchaser before a sale can be made I mean that the prospective purchaser's mind must be credulous. A state of confidence must have been established and it is obvious that there can be no set rule for either establishing confidence or neutralizing the mind to a state of openness. Here the ingenuity of the salesman must supply that which cannot be set down as a hard and fast rule.

I know a life insurance salesman who sells nothing but large policies, amounting to $100,000.00 and upward. Before this man even approaches the subject of insurance with a prospective client he familiarizes himself with the prospective client's complete history, including his education, his financial status, his eccentricities if he has any, his religious preferences and other data too numerous to be listed. Armed with this information, he manages to secure an introduction under conditions which permit him to know the prospective client in a social as well as a business way. Nothing is said about the sale of life insurance during his first visit, nor his second, and sometimes he does not approach the subject of insurance until he has become very well acquainted with the prospective client.

All this time, however, he is not dissipating his efforts. He is taking advantage of these friendly visits for the purpose of neutralizing his prospective client's mind; that is, he is building up a relationship of confidence so that when the time comes for him to talk life insurance that which he says will fall upon ears that *willingly listen.*

Some years ago I wrote a book entitled *How to Sell Your Services.* Just before the manuscript went to the publisher, it occurred to me to request some of the well-known men of the United States to write letters of endorsement to be published in the book. The printer was then waiting for the manuscript; therefore, I hurriedly wrote a letter to some eight or ten men, in which I briefly outlined exactly what I wanted, but the letter brought back no replies. I had failed to observe two important prerequisites for success—I had written the letter so hurriedly that I had failed to inject the spirit of *enthusiasm* into it, and, I had neglected so to word the letter that it had the effect of neutralizing the minds of those to whom it was sent; therefore, I had not paved the way for the application of the principle of *suggestion.*

After I discovered my mistake, I then wrote a letter that was based upon strict application of the principle of *suggestion,* and this letter not only brought back replies from all to whom it was sent, but many of the replies were masterpieces and served, far beyond my fondest hopes, as valuable supplements to the book.

NOT ALL ADVICE IS GOOD ADVICE

Suggestion is one of the most subtle and powerful principles of psychology. You are making use of it in all that you do and say and think, but, unless you understand the difference between negative suggestion and positive suggestion, you may be using it in such a way that it is bringing you defeat instead of success.

Science has established the fact that through the negative use of suggestion life may be extinguished. Some years ago, in France, a criminal was condemned to death, but before the time for his execution an experiment was performed on him which conclusively proved that through the principle of suggestion death, could be produced. The criminal was brought to the guillotine and his head was placed under the knife, after he had been blindfolded. A heavy, sharp edged plank was then dropped on his neck, producing a shock similar to that of a sharp edged knife. Warm water was then gently poured on his neck and allowed to trickle slowly down his spine, to imitate the flow of warm blood. In seven minutes the doctors pronounced the man dead. His imagination, through the principle of suggestion, had actually turned the sharp edged plank into a guillotine blade and stopped his heart from beating.

In the little town where I was raised, there lived an old lady who constantly complained that she feared death from cancer. During her childhood she had seen a woman who had cancer and the sight had so impressed itself upon her mind that she began to look for the symptoms of cancer in her own body. She was sure that every little ache and pain was the beginning of her long- looked-for symptom of cancer. I have seen her place her hand on her breast and have heard her exclaim, "Oh, I am sure I have a cancer growing here. I can feel it." When complaining of this imaginary disease, she always placed her hand on her left breast, where she believed the cancer was attacking her.

For more than twenty years she kept this up.

A few weeks ago she died—*with cancer on her left breast!* If suggestion will actually turn the edge of a plank into a guillotine blade and transform healthy body cells into parasites out of which cancer will develop, can you not imagine what it will do in destroying disease germs, if properly directed? *Suggestion* is the law through which mental healers work what appear to be miracles. I have personally witnessed the removal of parasitical growths known as warts, through the aid of suggestion, within forty-eight hours.

You—the reader of this lesson—can be sent to bed with *imaginary* sickness of the worst sort, in two hours' time or less, through the use of *suggestion.* If you should start down the street and three or four people in whom you had confidence should meet you and each exclaim that you look ill you would be ready for a doctor.

I wish to take advantage of this appropriate opportunity to state that all of the really big men whom I have had the pleasure of knowing have been the most willing and courteous men of my acquaintance when it came to rendering service that was of benefit to others. Perhaps that was one reason why they were *really* big men.

THE HUMAN MIND IS A MARVELOUS PIECE OF MACHINERY!

One of its outstanding characteristics is noticed in the fact that all impressions which reach it, either through outside *suggestion* or Auto-suggestion, are recorded together in groups which harmonize in nature. The negative impressions are stored away, all in one portion of the brain, while the positive impressions are stored in another portion. When one of these impressions (or past experiences) is called into the conscious mind, through the principle of memory, there is a tendency to recall with it all others of a similar nature, just as the raising of one link of a chain brings up other links with it. For example, anything that causes a feeling of doubt to arise in a person's mind is sufficient to call forth all of his experiences which caused him to become doubtful. If a man is asked by a stranger to cash a check, immediately he remembers having cashed checks that were not good, or of having heard of others who did so. Through the law of association all similar emotions, experiences and sense impressions that reach the mind are filed away together, so that the recalling of one has a tendency to bring back to memory all the others.

To arouse a feeling of distrust in a person's mind has a tendency to bring to the surface every doubt-building experience that person ever had. For this reason successful salesmen endeavor to keep away from the discussion of subjects that may arouse the buyer's "chain of doubt impressions" which he has stored away by reason of previous experiences. The successful salesman quickly learns that "knocking" a competitor or a competing article may result in bringing to the buyer's mind certain negative emotions growing out of previous experiences which may make it impossible for the salesman to "neutralize" the buyer's mind.

This principle applies to and controls every sense impression that is lodged in the human mind. Take the feeling of fear, for example; the moment we permit a single emotion that is related to fear to reach the conscious mind, it calls with it all of its unsavory relations. A feeling of courage cannot claim the attention of the conscious mind while a feeling of fear is there. One or the other must dominate. They make poor roommates because they do not harmonize in nature. Like attracts like. Every thought held in the conscious mind has a tendency to draw to it other thoughts of a similar nature. You see, therefore, that these feelings, thoughts and emotions growing out of past experiences, which claim the attention of the conscious mind, are backed by a regular army of supporting soldiers of a similar nature, that stand ready to aid them in their work.

Deliberately place in your own mind, through the principle of Autosuggestion, the ambition to succeed through the aid of a *definite chief aim,* and notice how quickly all of your latent or undeveloped ability in the nature of past experiences will become stimulated and aroused to action in your behalf. Plant in a boy's mind, through the principle of *suggestion,* the ambition to become a successful lawyer or doctor or engineer or business man or financier, and if you plant that suggestion deeply enough, and keep it there, by repetition, it will begin to move that boy toward the achievement of the object of that ambition.

If you would plant a *suggestion* "deeply," mix it generously with *enthusiasm,* for enthusiasm is the fertilizer that will insure its rapid growth as well as its permanency.

When that kind-hearted old gentleman planted in my mind the suggestion that I was a "bright boy" and that I could make my mark in the world if I would educate myself, it was not so much *what* he said, as it was the *way in which he said it* that made such a deep and lasting impression on my mind. It was the way in which he gripped my shoulders and the look of confidence in his eyes that drove his suggestion so deeply into my subconscious mind that it never gave me any peace until I commenced taking the steps that led to the fulfillment of the suggestion.

This is a point that I would stress with all the power at my command. *It is not so much what you say as it is the TONE and MANNER in which you say it that makes, a lasting impression.*

It naturally follows, therefore, that sincerity of purpose, honesty and earnestness must be placed back of all that one says if one would make a lasting and favorable impression.

Whatever you successfully sell to others you must first sell to *yourself.*

POINTS TO REMEMBER

1. Enthusiasm is the vital moving force that impels *action.*
2. Thoughts can be influenced through suggestion and autosuggestion.
3. Happiness is the final object of all human effort.

5

HABIT OF DOING MORE THAN PAID FOR

There are many objects, motives and people which arouse one's love-nature. There is some work which we do not like, some that we do like moderately, and, under certain conditions, there may be work that we actually LOVE!

Great artists, for example, generally love their work. The day laborer, on the other hand, usually not only dislikes his work, but may actually hate it.

Work which one does merely for the sake of earning a living is seldom liked. More often it is disliked, or even hated.

When engaged in work which he loves, a man may labor for an unbelievably long period of hours without becoming fatigued. Work that a man dislikes or hates brings on fatigue very quickly.

A man's endurance, therefore, depends very largely on the extent to which he likes, dislikes or loves that which he is doing.

We are here laying the foundation, as you will of course observe, for the statement of one of the most important laws of this philosophy, viz.:

A man is most efficient and will more quickly and easily succeed when engaged in work that he loves, or work that he performs in behalf of some person whom he loves.

Whenever the element of love enters into any task that one performs, the quality of the work becomes immediately improved and the quantity increased, without a corresponding increase in the fatigue caused by the work.

Some years ago a group of socialists, or perhaps they called themselves "co-operators," organized a colony in Louisiana, purchased several hundred acres of farm land, and started to work out an ideal which they believed would give them greater happiness in life and fewer of the worries through a system that provided each person with work at the sort of labor he liked best.

Their idea was to pay no wages to anyone. Each person did the work he liked best, or that for which he might be best equipped, and the products of their combined labors became the property of all. They had their own dairy, their own brick-making plant, their own cattle, poultry, etc. They had their own schools and a printing plant through which they published a paper.

A Swedish gentleman from Minnesota joined the colony, and at his own request he was placed at work in the printing plant. Very soon he complained that he did not like the work, so he was changed and put to work on the farm, operating a tractor. Two days of this was all he could stand, so he again applied for a transfer, and was assigned to the dairy. He could not get along with the cows, so he was once more changed, to the laundry, where he lasted but one day. One by one he tried every job on the works, but liked none of them. It had begun to look as if he did not fit in with the co-operative idea of living, and he was about to withdraw when someone happened to think of one job he had not yet tried—in the brick plant, so he was given a wheelbarrow and put to work wheeling bricks from the kilns and stacking them in piles, in the brick yard. A week's time went by and no complaint was registered by him. When asked if he liked his job he replied, "This ban chust the job I like."

Imagine anyone preferring a job wheeling bricks! However, that job suited the Swede's nature, he worked alone, at a task which called for no thought, and placed upon him no responsibility, which was just what he wanted.

He remained at the job until all the bricks had been wheeled out and stacked, then withdrew from the colony because there was no more brick work to be done. "The nice quiet job ban finished, so I yank I ban go back to Minney-so-tie," and back to "Minney-sotie" he went!

When a man is engaged in work that he loves it is no hardship for him to do more work and better work than that for which he is paid, and for this very reason every man owes it to himself to do his best to find the sort of work he likes best.

I have a perfect right to offer this advice to the students of this philosophy for the reason that I have followed it, myself, without reason to regret having done so.

This seems to be an appropriate place to inject a little personal history concerning both the author and the Law of Success philosophy, the purpose of which is to show that labor performed in a spirit of love for the sake of the labor, itself, never has been and never will be lost.

This entire lesson is devoted to the offering of evidence that it really pays to render more service and better service than one is paid to render. What an empty and useless effort this would be if the author had not, himself, practiced this rule long enough to be able to say just how it works out.

For over a quarter of a century I have been engaged in the labor of love out of which this philosophy has been developed, and I am perfectly sincere when I repeat that which I have stated elsewhere in this course, that I have been amply paid for my labors, by the pleasure I have had as I went along, even if I received nothing more.

My labors on this philosophy made it necessary, many years ago, for me to choose between immediate monetary returns, which I might have enjoyed by directing my efforts along purely commercial lines, and remuneration that comes in later years, and which is represented by both the usual financial standards and other forms of pay which can be measured only in terms of accumulated knowledge that enables one to enjoy the world about him more keenly.

The man who engages in work that he loves best does not always have the support, in his choice, of his closest friends and relatives.

Combating negative suggestions from friends and relatives has required an alarming proportion of my energies, during the years that I have been engaged in research work for the purpose of gathering, organizing, classifying and testing the material which has gone into this course.

These personal references are made solely for the purpose of showing the students of this philosophy that seldom, if ever, can one hope to engage in the work one loves best without meeting with obstacles of some nature. Generally, the chief obstacles in the way of one engaging in the sort of work one loves best is that it may not be the work which brings the greatest remuneration at the start.

To offset this disadvantage, however, the one who engages in the sort of work he loves is generally rewarded with two very decided benefits, namely; first, he usually finds in such work the greatest of all rewards, HAPPINESS, which is priceless, and secondly, his actual reward in money, when averaged over a lifetime of effort, is generally much greater, for the reason that labor which is performed in a spirit of love is usually greater in quantity and finer in quality than that which is performed solely for money.

DON'T DO MORE WORK, BUT BETTER WORK

There are more than a score of sound reasons why you should develop the habit of performing more service and *better service* than that for which you are paid, despite the fact that a large majority of the people are not rendering such service.

There are two reasons, however, for rendering such service, which transcend, in importance, all the others; namely,

First: By establishing a reputation as being a person who always renders more service and better service than that for which you are paid, you will benefit by comparison with those around you who do not render such service, and the contrast will be so noticeable that *there will be keen competition for your services, no matter what your life-work may be.*

It would be an insult to your intelligence to offer proof of the soundness of this statement, because it is obviously sound. Whether you are preaching sermons, practicing law, writing books, teaching school, or digging ditches, you will become more valuable and you will be able to command greater pay the minute you gain recognition as a person who does more than that for which he is paid.

Second: By far the most important reason why you should render more service than that for which you are paid; a reason that is basic and fundamental in nature; may be described in this way: Suppose that you wished to develop a strong right arm, and suppose that you tried to do so by tying the arm to your side with a rope, thus taking it out of use and giving it a long rest. Would disuse bring strength, or would it bring atrophy and weakness, resulting, finally, in your being compelled to have the arm removed?

You know that if you wished a strong right arm you could develop such an arm *only by giving it the hardest sort of use.* Take a look at the arm of a blacksmith if you wish to know how an arm may be made strong. Out of resistance comes strength. The strongest oak tree of the forest is not the one that is protected from the storm and hidden from the sun, but it is the one that stands in the open, where it is compelled to struggle for its existence against the winds and rains and the scorching sun.

It is through the operation of one of Nature's unvarying laws that struggle and resistance develop strength, and the purpose of this lesson is to show you how to harness this law and so use it that it will aid you in your struggle for success. By performing more service and better service than that for which you are paid, you not only exercise your service-rendering qualities, and thereby develop skill and ability of an extraordinary sort, but you build reputation that is valuable. If you form the habit of rendering such service you will become so adept in your work that you can *command* greater remuneration than those who do not perform such service. You will eventually develop sufficient strength to enable you to remove yourself from any undesirable station in life, and no one can or will desire to stop you.

If you are an employee you can make yourself so valuable, through this habit of performing more service than that for which you are paid, that you can practically set your own wages and no sensible employer will try to stop you. If your employer should be so unfortunate as to try to withhold from you the compensation to which you are entitled, this will not long remain as a handicap because other employers will discover this unusual quality and offer you employment.

The very fact that most people are rendering as little service as they can possibly get by with serves as an advantage to all who are rendering more service than that for which they are paid, because it enables all who do this to profit by comparison. You can "get by" if you render as little service as possible, but that is all you will get; and when work is slack and retrenchment sets in, you will be one of the first to be dismissed.

For more than twenty-five years I have carefully studied men with the object of ascertaining why some achieve noteworthy success while others with just as much ability do not get ahead; and it seems significant that every person whom I have observed applying this principle of rendering more service than that for which he was paid, was holding a better position and receiving more pay than those who merely performed sufficient service to "get by" with.

Personally I never received a promotion in my life that I could not trace directly to recognition that I had gained try rendering more service and better service than that for which I was paid.

I am stressing the importance of making this principle a habit as a means of enabling an employee to promote himself to a higher position, with greater pay, for the reason that this course will be studied by thousands of young men and young women who work for others. However, the principle applies to the employer or to the professional man or woman just the same as to the employee.

Observance of this principle brings a two-fold reward. First, it brings the reward of greater material gain than that enjoyed by those who do not observe it; and, second, it brings that reward of happiness and satisfaction which come only to those who render such service. If you receive no pay except that which comes in your pay envelope, you are underpaid, no matter how much money that envelope contains.

◆

My wife has just returned from the Public Library with a book for me to read. The book is entitled *Observation; Every Man His Own University*, by Russell H. Conwell.

By chance I opened this book at the beginning of the chapter entitled Every Man's University, and, as I read it through, my first impulse was to recommend that you go to the Public Library and read the entire book; but, upon second thought, I will not do this; instead, I will recommend that you purchase the book and read it, not once but a hundred times, because it covers the subject of this lesson as though it had been written for that purpose; covers it in a far more impressive manner than I could do it.

The following quotation from the chapter entitled Every Man's University will give you an idea of the golden nugget of truth to be found throughout the book:

> The intellect can be made to look far beyond the range of what men and women ordinarily see, but not all the colleges in the world can alone confer this power—this is the reward of *self-culture;* each must acquire it for himself; and perhaps this is why the power of observing deeply and widely is so much oftener found in those men and those women who have never crossed the threshold of any college but the *University of Hard Knocks.*

Read that book as a part of this lesson, because it will prepare you to profit by the philosophy and psychology upon which the lesson is built.

THE LAW OF INCREASING RETURNS!

Let us begin our analysis by showing how Nature employs this law in behalf of the tillers of the soil. The farmer carefully prepares the ground, then sows his wheat and waits while the Law of Increasing Returns brings back the seed he has sown, *plus a many-fold increase.*

But for this Law of Increasing Returns, man would perish, because he could not make the soil produce sufficient food for his existence. There would be no advantage to be gained by sowing a field of wheat if the harvest yield did not return more than was sown.

With this vital "tip" from Nature, which we may gather from the wheat fields, let us proceed to appropriate this Law of Increasing Returns and learn how to apply it to the service we render, to the end that *it may yield returns in excess of and out of proportion to the effort put forth.*

First of all, let us emphasize the fact that there is no trickery or chicanery connected with this Law, although quite a few seem not to have learned this great truth, judging by the number who spend all of their efforts either trying to get something for nothing, or something for less than its true value.

It is to no such end that we recommend the use of the Law of Increasing Returns, for no such end is possible, within the broad meaning of the word success.

Another remarkable and noteworthy feature of the Law of Increasing Returns is the fact that it may be used by those who purchase service with as great returns as it can be by those who render service, for Proof of which we have but to study the effects of Henry Ford's famous Five-Dollar-a-day minimum wage scale which he inaugurated some years ago.

Those who are familiar with the facts say that Mr. Ford was

not playing the part of a philanthropist when he inaugurated this minimum wage scale; but, to the contrary, he was merely taking advantage of a sound business principle which has probably yielded him greater returns, in both dollars and goodwill, than any other single policy ever inaugurated at the Ford plant.

By paying more wages than the average, he received more service and better service than the average!

At a single stroke, through the inauguration of that minimum wage policy, Ford attracted the best labor on the market and placed a premium upon the privilege of working in his plant.

I have no authentic figures at hand bearing on the subject, but I have sound reason to conjecture that for every five dollars Ford spent, under this policy, he received at least seven dollars and fifty cents' worth of service. I have, also, sound reason to believe that this policy enabled Ford to reduce the cost of supervision, because employment in his plant became so desirable that no worker would care to run the risk of losing his position by "soldiering" on the job or rendering poor service.

Where other employers were forced to depend upon costly supervision in order to get the service to which they were entitled, and for which they were paying, Ford got the same or better service by the less expensive method of placing a premium upon employment in his plant.

Marshall Field was probably the leading merchant of his time, and the great Field store, in Chicago, stands today as a monument to his ability to apply the Law of Increasing Returns.

A customer purchased an expensive lace waist at the Field store, but did not wear it. Two years later she gave it to her niece as a wedding present. The niece quietly returned the waist to the Field store and exchanged it for other merchandise, despite the fact that it had been out for more than two years and was then out of style.

Not only did the Field store take back the waist, but, what is of more importance it did so *without argument!*

Of course there was no obligation, moral or legal, on the part of the store to accept the return of the waist at that late date, which makes the transaction all the more significant.

The waist was originally priced at fifty dollars, and of course it had to be thrown on the bargain counter and sold for whatever it would bring, but the keen student of human nature will understand that the Field store not only did not lose anything on the waist, but it actually profited by the transaction to an extent that cannot be measured in mere dollars.

The woman who returned the waist knew that she was not entitled to a rebate; therefore, when the store gave her that to which she was not entitled the transaction won her as a permanent customer. But the effect of the transaction did not end here; it only began; for this woman spread the news of the "fair treatment" she had received at the Field store, far and near. It was the talk of the women of her set for many days, and the Field store received more advertising from the transaction than it could have purchased in any other way with ten times the value of the waist.

The success of the Field store was built largely upon Marshall Field's understanding of the Law of Increasing Returns, which prompted him to adopt, as a part of his business policy, the slogan, "The customer is always right."

When you do only that for which you are paid, there is nothing out of the ordinary to *attract favorable comment* about the transaction; but, when you willingly do more than that for which you are paid, your action attracts the favorable attention of all who are affected by the transaction, and goes another step toward establishing a reputation that will eventually set the Law of Increasing Returns to work in your behalf, for this reputation will create a demand for your services, far and wide.

Carol Downes went to work for W. C. Durant, the automobile manufacturer, in a minor position. He is now Mr. Durant's right-hand man, and the president of one of his automobile distributing companies. He promoted himself into this profitable position solely through the aid of the Law of Increasing Returns, which he put into operation by rendering more service and better service than that for which he was paid.

In a recent visit with Mr. Downes I asked him to tell me how he managed to gain promotion so rapidly, in a few brief sentences he told the whole story.

"When I first went to work with Mr. Durant," said he, "I noticed that he always remained at the office long after all the others had gone home for the day, and I made it my business to stay there, also. No one asked me to stay, but I thought someone should be there to give Mr. Durant any assistance he might need. Often he would look around for someone to bring him a letter file, or render some other trivial service, and *always he found me there ready to serve him.* He got into the habit of calling on me; that is about all there is to the story."

"He got into the habit of calling on me!"

Read that sentence again, for it is full of meaning of the richest sort.

Why did Mr. Durant get into the habit of calling on Mr. Downes? Because *Mr Downes made it his business to be on hand where he would be seen.* He deliberately placed himself in Mr. Durant's way in order that he might render service that would place the Law of Increasing Returns back of him.

Was he told to do this? *No!*

Was he paid to do it? *Yes!* He was paid by the opportunity

it offered for him to bring himself to the attention of the man who had it within his power to promote him.

We are now approaching the most important part of this lesson, because this is an appropriate place at which to suggest that *you* have the same opportunity to make use of the Law of Increasing Returns that Mr. Downes had, and you can go about the application of the Law in exactly the same way that he did, *by being on hand and ready to volunteer your services in the performance of work which others may shirk because they are not paid to do it.*

Stop! Don't say it—don't even think it if you have the slightest intention of springing that old timeworn phrase entitled, "But my *employer is different.*"

Of course he is different. All men are different in most respects, but they are very much alike in this—they are somewhat *selfish;* in fact they are selfish enough not to want a man such as Carol Downes to cast his lot with their competitor, and this very selfishness may be made to serve you as an asset and not as a liability *if—*

You have the good judgment to make yourself so useful that the person to whom you sell your services cannot get along without you.

One of the most advantageous promotions I ever received came about through an incident which seemed so insignificant that it appeared to be unimportant. One Saturday afternoon, a lawyer, whose office was on the same floor as that of my employer, came in and asked if I knew where he could get a stenographer to do some work which he was compelled to finish that day.

I told him that all of our stenographers had gone to the ball game, and that I would have been gone had he called five minutes later, but that I would be very glad to stay and do his work as I could go to a ball game any day and his work had to be done then.

I did the work for him, and when he asked how much he owed me I replied, "Oh, about a thousand dollars, as long as it is you; if it were for anyone else, I wouldn't charge anything." He smiled, and thanked me.

Little did I think, when I made that remark, that he would ever pay me a thousand dollars for that afternoon's work, but *he did!* Six months later, after I had entirely forgotten the incident, he called on me again, and asked how much salary I was receiving. When I told him he informed me that he was ready to pay me that thousand dollars which I had laughingly said I would charge him for the work I had performed for him and he *did pay it* by giving me a position at a thousand dollars a year increase in salary.

Unconsciously, I had put the Law of Increasing Returns to work in my behalf that afternoon, by giving up the ball game and rendering a service which was obviously rendered out of a desire to be helpful and not for the sake of a monetary consideration.

It was not my duty to give up my Saturday afternoon, but—

It was my *privilege!*

Furthermore, it was a profitable privilege, because it yielded me a thousand dollars in cash and a much more responsible position than the one I had formerly occupied.

It was Carol Downes' *duty* to be on hand until the usual quitting time, but it was his *privilege* to remain at his post after the other workers had gone, and that privilege properly exercised brought him greater responsibilities and a salary that yields him more in a year than he would have made in a lifetime in the position he occupied before he exercised the privilege.

I have been thinking for more than twenty-five years of

this *privilege* of performing more service and better service than that for which we are paid, and my thoughts have led me to the conclusion that a single hour devoted each day to rendering service for which we are not paid, can be made to yield bigger returns than we received from the entire remainder of the day the day during which we are merely performing our *duty*.

◆

By the very nature of the subject of this lesson it can never be finished, for it leads into the heart of all human activities. Its purpose is to cause you to take the fundamentals upon which it is based and use them as a stimulus that will cause your mind to unfold, thereby releasing the latent forces that are yours.

This lesson was not written for the purpose of teaching you, but it was intended as a means of causing you to teach yourself one of the great truths of life. It was intended as a source of education, in the true sense of educing, drawing out, developing from within, those forces of mind which are available for your use.

When you deliver the best service of which you are capable, striving each time to excel all your previous efforts, you are making use of the highest form of education. Therefore, when you render more service and better service than that for which you are paid, you, more than anyone else, are profiting by the effort.

It is only through the delivery of such service that mastery in your chosen field of endeavor can be attained. For this reason you should make it a part of your *definite chief aim* to endeavor to surpass all previous records in all that you do. Let this become a part of your daily habits, and follow it with the same regularity with which you eat your meals.

Make it your business to render more service and better

service than that for which you are paid, and lo! before you realize what has happened, you will find that THE WORLD IS WILLINGLY PAYING YOU FOR MORE THAN YOU DO!

Compound interest upon compound interest is the rate that you will be paid for such service. Just how this pyramiding of gains takes place is left entirely to you to determine.

Now, what are you going to do with that which you have learned from this lesson? and when? and how? and why? This lesson can be of no value to you unless it moves you to adopt and use the knowledge it has brought you.

Knowledge becomes POWER only through organization and USE! Do not forget this.

You can never become a Leader without doing more than you are paid for, and you cannot become successful without developing leadership in your chosen occupation.

POINTS TO REMEMBER

1. Every man owes it to himself to do his best to find the sort of work he likes best.
2. By performing more services than that you are paid, you can set your own goals.
3. Apply the Law of Increasing Returns.

6

AUTOSUGGESTION

Autosuggestion is a term which applies to all suggestions and all self-administered stimuli which reach one's mind through the five senses. Stated in another way, autosuggestion is *self-suggestion*. It is the agency of communication between that part of the mind where conscious thought takes place and that which serves as the seat of action for the subconscious mind.

The dominating thoughts which one *permits* to remain in the conscious mind (whether these thoughts be negative or positive is immaterial) will *reach and influence* the subconscious mind, through the Law of Autosuggestion.

NO THOUGHT, whether it be negative or positive, CAN ENTER THE SUBCONSCIOUS MIND WITHOUT THE AID OF THE PRINCIPLE OF AUTOSUGGESTION, with the exception of those thoughts picked up as "flashes of insight or inspiration." Stated differently, all sense impressions which are perceived through the five senses are captured and processed by the *conscious* thinking mind and may be either passed on to the *subconscious* mind or rejected, at will. The conscious faculty serves, therefore, as an outer guard at the approach to the subconscious.

Nature has so "wired" human beings that they have ABSOLUTE CONTROL over the material which reaches their subconscious mind through the five senses, although this is not meant to be construed as a statement that individuals always EXERCISE this control. In the great majority of instances, they do NOT exercise it, which explains why so many people go through life in poverty.

Your ability to use the Law of Autosuggestion will depend very largely upon your capacity to CONCENTRATE upon a given DESIRE until that desire becomes a BURNING OBSESSION.

Here is a most significant fact—the subconscious mind takes any orders given it in a spirit of absolute FAITH, and acts upon those orders, although the orders often have to be presented *over and over again*, through repetition, before they are interpreted by the subconscious mind. Consider the possibility of playing a perfectly legitimate trick on your subconscious mind by making it believe, *because you believe it*, that you must have the amount of money you are visualizing, that this money is already awaiting your claim, that the subconscious mind MUST hand over to you practical plans for acquiring the money which is yours.

Hand over the thought suggested in the preceding paragraph to your IMAGINATION and see what your imagination can, or will do, to create practical plans for the accumulation of money through transmutation of your desire.

DO NOT WAIT for a definite plan through which you intend to exchange services or merchandise in return for the money you are visualizing, but begin at once to see yourself in possession of the money, DEMANDING and EXPECTING meanwhile that your subconscious mind will hand over the plan or plans you need. Be on the alert for these plans, and when they appear, put them into ACTION IMMEDIATELY. When the plans appear, they will probably flash into your mind through the sixth sense, in the form of an inspiration. This inspiration may be considered a direct "telegram" or "message" from Infinite Intelligence. Treat it with respect, and act upon it as soon as you receive it. Failure to do this will be FATAL to your success.

SUMMARY OF INSTRUCTIONS

The fact that you are reading this book is an indication that you earnestly seek knowledge. It is also an indication that you are a student of this subject. If you are only a student, there is a chance you may learn much that you did not know, but you will learn only by assuming an attitude of humility. If you choose to follow some of the instructions, but neglect or refuse to follow others—*you will fail!* To get satisfactory results, you must follow ALL instructions in a spirit of FAITH.

The instructions given in connection with the six action steps in Chapter I will now be summarized and blended with the principles covered by this chapter. If your DEFINITE CHIEF AIM involves money and the attainment of wealth:

First: Go into some quiet spot (preferably in bed at night) where you will not be disturbed or interrupted, close your eyes, and repeat aloud (so you may hear your own words) the written statement of the amount of money you intend to accumulate, the time limit for its accumulation, and a description of the service or merchandise you intend to give in return for the money.

As you carry out these instructions, SEE YOURSELF ALREADY IN POSSESSION OF THE MONEY.

For example, suppose that you intend to accumulate $500,000 by the first of January, five years hence, that you intend to give personal services in return for the money in the capacity of a sales representative. Your written statement of your purpose should be similar to the following:

"By the first day of January, [here state the year], I will have in my possession $500,000, which will come to me in various amounts from time to time during the interim.

"In return for this money I will give the most efficient service of which I am capable, rendering the fullest possible quantity, and the best possible quality of service in the capacity of selling… (describe the service or merchandise you intend to sell).

"I believe that I will have this money in my possession. My faith is so strong that I can now see this money before my eyes. I can touch it with my hands. It is now awaiting transfer to me at the time and in the proportion that I deliver the service I intend to render in return for it. I am awaiting a plan by which to accumulate this money, and I will follow that plan when it is received."

Second: Repeat this program night and morning until you can clearly visualize (in your imagination) the money you intend to accumulate.

Third: Place a written copy of your statement where you can see it night and morning, and read it just before retiring and upon arising until it has been memorized.

Remember as you carry out these instructions that you are applying the Law of Autosuggestion for the purpose of giving orders to your subconscious mind. Remember that these instructions apply particularly to the desire for money, but also to any other object you desire or goal you seek. Remember also that your subconscious mind will act ONLY upon instructions which are emotionalized and handed over to it with feeling. FAITH is the strongest and most productive of the emotions.

These instructions may at first seem abstract. Do not let this disturb you. Follow the instructions no matter how abstract or impractical they may at first appear to be. The time will soon come, if you do as you have been instructed, *in spirit as well as in fact*, when a whole new universe of power will unfold to you.

Skepticism, in connection with ALL new ideas, is characteristic of all human beings. But if you follow the instructions outlined, your skepticism will soon be replaced by belief, and this in turn will soon become crystallized into ABSOLUTE FAITH. Then you will have arrived at the point where you may truly say, "I am the Master of my Fate, I am the Captain of my Soul!"

Many philosophers have made the statement that each person is the master of his or her own earthly destiny, but most of them have failed to say why this is so. The reason that we may be the master of our own earthly status, and especially our financial status, is thoroughly explained in this chapter. We may become the master of ourselves, and of our environment, because we have the POWER TO INFLUENCE OUR OWN SUBCONSCIOUS MIND, and through it, to gain the cooperation of Infinite Intelligence.

The chapter you are now reading represents the keystone in the arch of *The Think and Grow Rich Philosophy*. The instructions contained in this chapter must be understood and APPLIED WITH PERSISTENCE if you are to succeed in transmuting desire into money or any other result you seek.

The actual performance of transmuting DESIRE into money involves the use of autosuggestion as an agency by which you may reach and influence the subconscious mind. The other principles are simply tools with which to apply autosuggestion. Keep this thought in mind, and you will at all times be conscious of the important part that the Law of Autosuggestion is to play in your efforts to accumulate money through the methods described in this book.

Carry out these instructions as though you were a small child. Inject into your efforts something of the FAITH of a child. I have been most careful to see that no impractical instructions are included because of my sincere desire to be helpful.

After you have read the entire book, come back to this chapter and follow in spirit, and in action, this instruction:

READ THIS ENTIRE CHAPTER ALOUD ONCE EVERY NIGHT UNTIL YOU BECOME THOROUGHLY CONVINCED THAT THE PRINCIPLE OF AUTOSUGGESTION IS SOUND, THAT IT WILL ACCOMPLISH FOR YOU ALL THAT HAS BEEN CLAIMED FOR IT. AS YOU READ, *UNDERSCORE WITH A PENCIL* EVERY SENTENCE WHICH IMPRESSES YOU FAVORABLY.

Follow the foregoing instructions to the letter and it will open the way for a complete understanding and mastery of all the principles of success.

POINTS TO REMEMBER

1. Your ability to use the Law of Autosuggestion will depend largely upon your capacity to concentrate.
2. Faith is the strongest and most productive of the emotions.
3. Use your power to influence your own subconscious mind.

7

CLOSE THE DOORS ON YOUR PAST

Whenever you meet a misfortune, put it into your past. Keep your mind upon future achievement, and you will find that mistakes of the past often work to fill the future with good fortune. Your wealth and your peace of mind are strongly connected with each other. Even at the lowest-level jobs, your success waits within your own mind. Add value to your work and you set in motion the forces that make the concepts of your mind turn into the realities of living.

When I was still a poor youth in Wise County, Virginia, I invested twenty-five cents in a raffle ticket. The prize was a horse—and I won! A horse was of considerable value to a farming family in those days, and this one, all agreed, was a good horse. Filled with pride, I led him home. How fortunate I was!

Or was I? Having installed my horse carefully in the stable, I treated him to oats, corn and hay—all he could eat. That same night he broke out of the stable, went down to the river and drank his fill of water. As anyone who knows horses could have predicted, the poor bloated animal foundered and died. It cost me five dollars to have him hauled away and buried. So much for my good luck!

Yet who can tell the uses of the past? I was able in later years to look back upon that incident and see I had been fortunate. You see, I never again have been tempted to risk money in any kind of gambling. Surely I have saved the cost of many horses, let alone saved my peace of mind.

Now let me tell you of a more serious incident which cost a man's life, threatened my own life, prevented me from taking advantage of a great opportunity, seemed like an unmitigated disaster—and yet turned out to be for my boundless good and the good of others as well.

At that time I had completed the first draft of *The Science of Personal Achievement*, in eight volumes, and I needed a publisher. Mr. Don R. Mellett, publisher of the Canton, Ohio Daily News, became my partner and business manager. We induced Judge Elbert H. Gary, Chairman of the Board of the United States Steel Corporation, to supply the money necessary to print the first edition. Furthermore, Judge Gary agreed to purchase a complete set of the books for every key man employed in that vast corporation. The contract had not yet been signed, but I was on top of the world.

Now, Mr. Mellett had been using his newspaper as a means to expose a very unholy alliance between the bootleggers and the police force of his city. Three days before we were to meet Judge Gary, a member of the police force and a gangster shot and killed Don Mellett. Because I had been associated with him, the gang believed I too had had something to do with their exposure. I missed assassination by only a few hours.

For a year I had to hide. At length the murderers were caught, convicted and given lifetime sentences in prison. Meanwhile Judge Gary had died. All my plans were upset, I had had to waste much precious time while in hiding, and I had no publisher. I was right back where I had started—or rather, I was behind where I had been.

I made a new start and found a publisher for my writings. That is a story in itself, but it is not the point of this story.

I found out later that if Judge Gary had become my financial backer, and if *The Science of Personal Achievement* had been distributed within the United States Steel Corporation as had been planned, I would forever after have been looked upon as a tool of Big Business. *The Science of Personal Achievement* would have been greeted with suspicion, would have been turned down cold by many of those whom it now serves. Furthermore, I might have been inhibited against making statements I have made from time to time against Big Business when it forgets its real purpose, which is to build a better world for mankind.

Every adversity has within it the seed of an equivalent or a greater benefit. Can you remember that? Write it on a card. Carry the card in your pocket and read it daily! In that phrase lies the key to many a man's peace of mind. It is not the Supreme Secret to which I have referred but it lives on the same street. Set it firmly into your consciousness: Every adversity has within it the seed of an equivalent or a greater benefit.

Thus it is possible, and strongly advisable, to CLOSE THE DOORS TO YOUR PAST insofar as any regrets or bitterness or post-mortems are concerned. You are searching for wealth and peace of mind. Neither the way to wealth nor the way to peace of mind leads through the graveyard of unpleasant experiences long past.

When you have attained peace of mind, your mind will automatically reject every thought and every mental reaction which is not beneficial to your welfare. Meanwhile, help yourself attain this great command-of-mind and all it can do for you. Avoid all negative mental influences and especially avoid that shadow of mournful regret which can keep all the sunshine out of your life—and keep out other gold as well.

TIME—THE GREATEST HEALER

Time is the great magician. Close the door on ugly experiences, disappointments and frustrations! Then the great magician, Time, can transmute past sorrows and mistakes into present rewards, success and happiness.

Knut Hamsun, a Norwegian immigrant, failed at everything he tried in this country. In desperation he decided to write the story of his struggles. His book, which he called *Hunger*, won the Nobel Prize for literature. Hamsun's terrible experiences at length had made him a rich and famous man.

Harry S. Truman failed as a haberdasher. If, from then on, he had considered himself a failure, he certainly could not have entered upon the road to the presidency.

We have also the example of another man who took up storekeeping; but the store failed.

He took up engineering and also failed. The sheriff sold his surveying instruments to pay his debts.

He joined a group of soldiers in an Indian war and had the rank of captain. His record as a soldier was so poor that he was reduced to the rank of private and sent home.

He was passionately in love and engaged to be married. The girl died and left him in a terrible state of shock.

He took up law. He won few cases.

He went into politics, ran for office and was defeated.

Is it astonishing that Abraham Lincoln eventually became President? In a way it is and in a way it is not. He might have allowed his mind to drag failure and discouragement after him, as a prisoner drags his chains. After all, so many people do—and they are indeed prisoners of the past, never able to break free of the image of failure which, to them, means me.

He did not do this, however. The way in which he determinedly left failure behind him was no miracle—it is a grand privilege available to every human being. The man who became President had been tempered in the fires of life, or he could not have been what he was nor have done what he did.

You cannot see all of the great Plan of your life. You can make it full and rewarding, however, if you treat each sorrow and setback as a tempering toward greater and richer experiences to come.

Let me suggest:

Keep yourself aware of life's endless combinations of circumstances.

Have you been disappointed in love? Your heart feels literally broken. You can see no joy in the world. You may wish to take an overdose of sleeping pills and end it all. Yet is it likely that nowhere in the world exists the woman (or man) who can take the place of the one you lost? A moment of thought within the citadel of your deepest mind will show you this is hardly possible.

So it happened with me, for after a dreadful disappointment of the heart I met a combination of circumstances which led at last to the perfect wife. There is a more poignant point to the story. When, after a violent lover's quarrel, my first sweetheart turned away from me, married another man, I thought the world had ended. Five years later the man she married committed suicide, unbalanced by the constant friction of living with the woman I had been so anxious to marry. Where would I have been with a terror of a woman who heckled me instead of helping me?

Every adversity has within it the seed of an equivalent or greater benefit.

Remember that even a condition which the world calls HANDICAP you can call BENEFIT—and make it truly so.

I have mentioned that Thomas A. Edison had little formal schooling. W. Clement Stone, the highly successful insurance man, was a high school dropout. So many men have succeeded despite the lack of "book learning" that, without in the least downgrading education, we may say the lack of it need not be a handicap. It depends on the man.

But what of Edison's deafness? Surely a very marginal ability to hear is a handicap. But again it depends on the man.

Edison as a boy had been a "candy butcher" on trains. Once a man lifted him and his entire load of candy onto a train by his ears—and that was the beginning of the end of his hearing. He could have dwelt all his life on this cruel and damaging experience. Like many another, he could have put his major energies into bewailing his fate; but he didn't.

When I visited him, he was dependent upon a hearing aid—a primitive thing by today's standards. When I was sure we understood each other's minds I asked him if he had not found his deafness a great handicap. He replied:

"To the contrary, deafness has been a great help to me. It has saved me from having to listen to a lot of worthless chatter and it has taught me to hear from within."

Anyone who wants peace of mind should remember those last three words. By transmuting his affliction into a benefit, Mr. Edison learned how to tune in on all the subtle power which waits within every mind. He felt, too, that he heard, from within, the voice of an Infinite Intelligence and received guidance from an infallible Source.

Every adversity has within it the seed of an equivalent or greater benefit.

When you speak of failure, you attract failure. When you

speak of success, you attract success. I once made a survey of more than 30,000 men and women to ascertain their staying qualities in the face of failure and defeat.

For the majority of those people it took one—only one—setback to wed them to defeat.

Of those who kept on aspiring, another large percentage got started in various projects but quit even before meeting with defeat. The defeat came not from circumstances but from the built-in attitude of defeat which they carried from the past. Instead of closing the door on the past, they ran back through that door at every opportunity. Needless to say there were no Fords or Edisons in this group.

On the other hand, I am reminded of a man named Arthur Decio who built his career out of a family failure that had cost all of his father's savings. It was a business in mobile homes which never got going. Now the father handed it to the son, hopelessly. What could Decio, then in his twenties, do with the business? Most men would have liquidated it on the spot.

ILL FEELINGS CALL FOR ILL FATE

Starting in his garage next to the railroad tracks in Elkhart, Indiana, Mr. Decio first designed a small, easily transportable mobile home which research had shown him was needed. Later he applied General Motors methods in a business which never had known them before. He introduced frequent model changes. He built a network of dealers. He brought out four lines of mobile homes, each competing with the others. His company's sales in four years have increased 500 per cent, and Mr. Decio has made five million dollars out of the business that was about to fail.

Today's population includes a large proportion of youngmarrieds and retired couples, both groups being prime customers for mobile homes. Of course Mr. Decio realizes this, for every age has its special ways.

The many failures who turned up in my survey of some years ago displayed a failure-quality which belongs to any age. Not only had these people failed, but they kept on living with their failure. They spoke of it in preference to other topics. They lived in the past tense, reliving the pain of what had been.

Those who had succeeded, however, spoke in the future tense. Their eyes were not upon their past—which often contained a good share of mistakes—but ever upon the future, upon their great objectives. This too was the invariable case with those five hundred and more vastly successful men whom I interviewed at the behest of Andrew Carnegie. On their way up they talked "the way up." Where failure had been laid behind, failure stayed behind—and notably it stayed out of their conversation.

Concerning success and failure, I have observed another trait which has much to do with peace of mind.

It is obvious that those who are filled with malice and envy do not have peace of mind; their malice and envy sour their lives. Failure so often hates the very sight of success. Speaking with successful men, I have noticed they speak in complimentary terms of other men who are succeeding. Their attitude is not one of envy, but of willingness to learn from others. The failure, on the other hand, goes out of his way to find some adverse criticism of the successful person. If he can't find anything doubtful about the way that person does business, then he will pick at some other area. His malice is evident, and so is the sad fact that he not only cannot command what money can buy, but also he cannot attain peace of mind.

Is there a definite connection between being wealthy and having peace of mind? There is a connection, but it is not absolute. There certainly are poor people who have peace of mind; but they are far more rare than folklore would have us believe. You need not be a millionaire, but without sufficient money you are cut off from much in life that sustains the spirit. If you are continually worrying about where your next meal is to come from—when you'll be able to get your shoes repaired—how you are going to pay your dentist bill—how many more years your house can go without paint—you have no peace of mind. If your lack of funds forces you to live in a shabby neighborhood so that you constantly worry about the influence upon your children, you have no peace of mind. If you cannot occasionally buy and cherish something that is beautiful—if you cannot afford a vacation you really enjoy—if you cannot partake of a motion picture or a stage show which you know is very much worthwhile—your mind does not have the chance to satisfy itself. Money brings much good into your life and much that nobody should have to do without.

It is no surprise that there are many rich people who enjoy peace of mind. But there are many who do not. If the main purpose of a fortune is to make its possessor worry about keeping his fortune, peace of mind goes out the window.

One of the failures which have illuminated my knowledge and strengthened my soul came when I was quite wealthy. I simply became poor—quite poor. The circumstances are revealing.

Perhaps as a compensation for the dirt-poor days of my youth, I became enamored of big houses, big cars, lush acreage and similar symbols of wealth. Perhaps I was merely in line with my times, which seemed to demand that when a man had money, he had to display it. Today's millionaires are much less ostentatious.

At any rate, my books were selling well, I had made a name as a trainer of salesmen, other enterprises prospered—and so it seemed imperative that I must drive a Rolls-Royce. Soon I had a pair of Rolls-Royces. Soon after this, I cradled my cars in a big garage on a large estate in the Catskill Mountains, north of New York City. I saw that estate as a monument to my achievements.

The estate called for servants, for a maintenance staff, for foremen over the maintenance men. It called for lavish dinner parties, the expense of which would have made John D. Rockefeller groan. Once I gave out a general invitation to a barbecue dinner, expecting that perhaps a hundred people would show up. Over three thousand attended! The highway was tied up with a traffic jam for two miles each way, and the traffic patrolmen never did forgive me.

The clubhouse on the estate could sleep forty guests in comfort and was seldom without a full load. Once the overflow swept into my private quarters. I arrived home—hoping for some peace of mind—and found a stranger asleep in my bed.

Moreover, he had appropriated the only pair of pajamas I had available.

Let us draw the curtain on the Hill estate. It went for a song shortly after the crash of '29. When I got over the initial shock, how relieved I felt! How peaceful, how newly powerful was the mind which had been overlaid with worry!

Three of my friends, whose combined assets were less than the amount I lost when I lost my estate, did not have faith in the great principle that every adversity has within it the seed of an equivalent benefit. One jumped off a high building on Wall Street; one fired a bullet into his brain; and the third man was hauled out of the Hudson River six weeks after he had jumped in.

I made money again. Of course I did. The principles of the Science of Achievement saw to that. My lost estate had not lost with it my knowledge that any goal set up by a human mind can be achieved by that mind's possessor. Ever since, I have lived comfortably but without show. What good is money when it becomes a millstone?

Make sure your work and your money benefit someone besides yourself. One of the positive results that came after I had firmly closed the door on my experiences in the Catskill Mountains was this: I found time in which to write more books. These books have benefited me and they have benefited mankind—and so they have benefited me with more than money.

When Andrew Carnegie decided to use his great wealth to found free libraries, he greatly increased his peace of mind.

Henry Ford was pretty tough about giving away his money. When at length he learned it was possible to find people who deserved it and would use it well, I am sure he felt the same quiet satisfaction.

DON'T LET YOUR PAST OVERPOWER YOUR FUTURE

There is another important principle which insures that as your wealth grows, so will your peace of mind.

Do not hurt any other person in order that you may succeed. I am thankful I learned this early in life. When a man discovers himself and with it the ways in which he can earn big money, now and then he will see a way to put some extra weight on his side of the scales. Like the butcher's hand which is weighed along with the hamburger, it wouldn't be noticed. I could have added to my wealth by dishonest means on many an occasion, but I would have lost my peace of mind.

Among the men I interviewed after I accepted my commission from Andrew Carnegie were several who were little better than pirates of the business world. (In most cases I did not know this at the time.) Later events often showed how much they had given up when, in effect, they stole from others or ruthlessly ruined others in order to aggrandize themselves. Some went to prison. Some stayed out of prison on legal technicalities, but who has peace of mind when no honest man will look him in the face?

Today is the day of the large service corporation, often with a tremendous office staff. A man in a factory is likely to be judged by the kind of work he puts out, but a man in an office can push himself upward with various tricks of personality, tricks of paperwork, tricks of getting the other fellow to assume responsibility for mistakes, and so forth. To step up the ladder by stepping on another man's face is to make a mockery of the money you earn. There is no peace of mind in this and often there is no health, no ability to be happy, no harmony at home. You can be left with the ability to buy what money can buy—and a degree of unhappiness rather more acute than a beggar's.

I have spoken to several men in my classes who confessed they had cut many corners of honesty and business morality. Now they wished to make a new start—but was it possible? When they attained the only true wealth, honestly earned wealth, would they not still be made miserable by the tensions of guilt?

I assured them they would not if only they closed the door on the past. Let them consider dishonesty a mistake, even a disaster—but a past disaster.

This is an important point with many ramifications. Not necessarily dishonesty, but also any other negative state of mind held in the past can be left in the past just as one leaves physical circumstances.

I showed these men that now they were finding a new self. The past could not matter.

The world is full of examples of men who learned from their own bad consciences, or even in prison, that no dishonesty ever pays. The lesson learned is the lesson learned, and for most men there is time enough and world enough to start again and build a glorious future.

For an exception, I give you Al Capone. During the Great Depression, this notorious gangster set up free soup kitchens at which he fed numbers of the unemployed. He was fond of calling attention to these soup kitchens as proof of the good he was doing his fellow man. Of course I speak of no such mockeries.

Rather let us think of men like O. Henry, who served a jail sentence for a crime. Surely it helped him at last to find himself, for it was afterward that he became known for his wonderful stories with all their deep understanding of human nature.

Close the door on your past and keep it closed. I have heard it said that you never really get over the death of a loved one. This is so in the sense that every circumstance of your life, every joy and every sorrow, has an effect in shaping you into what you are. But you have great control over the way it shapes you—never forget that!

I am not one of those who believe in doing away with the

natural emotion of sorrow when death occurs. Tears and sorrow are provided by nature as a safety valve for the overflowing emotions. Yet most people wait too long to close the door on mourning; or they never close it. We say: "There is no use in worrying over something you can't control." Yet we worry over death for unconscionable periods of time, knowing all the while we cannot control it.

The physical body comes from the air and the soil and goes back to the sources from which it came. Perhaps the mental and spiritual portions and some mysterious essence of life also go back to sources we can sense but cannot discover. So be it! Carry along with you not the pain you knew when a loved one died, but rather the positive and sustaining memories. As life is a natural process, so death is also.

Do you think it is possible to have only one great love in your life, especially if that love was sealed in marriage? Human experience proves this is not so. While I believe firmly in marriage, I know that the word "marriage" is not always synonymous with the word "happiness." You have a right to happiness, and this is your life. When a marriage turns out to have been a mistake, when it can be broken but it is not broken, then the mistake is perpetuated and shadows all the rest of life. Sometimes the door of the past must be closed upon a marriage before either party to that marriage, or both, can find any kind of life-success.

A job that is past opens a new door to the future. Suppose you have lost your job through no fault of your own. Suppose, then, you nurse a great resentment and a festering hatred of your former employer who was so unjust to you. Meanwhile you are going around looking for another job—and something is saying No to any prospective future employer. What says No? The negative qualities of hatred and resentment which beam from your mind to his. He cannot tell just what it is, but he feels something disturbing about you and he doesn't want you in his office or his shop.

Put the temporary setback firmly behind you, however—go out with a determined will to get a better job than the one you lose—and anyone who interviews you will feel the positive qualities that mean good man. What if you are questioned about your former employer? Say nothing bad about him! What was bad must always stay in the past and never be allowed to hinder the future.

Jobs also seem to be favorite spots in which to grow grudges. Of course you have rights and it is no part of success or peace of mind to allow yourself to be stepped upon. Many little scratches in human relations, however, are nothing but that, just little scratches, and need not be reacted to as though they were deep wounds.

How BIG are you? It takes a big person to succeed. To begin with, it takes a big person to see what is big, and worth one's attention, rather than waste emotional energy on trifling matters. When you see how you damage yourself by bearing resentment and grudges, you can put small annoyances in the past as soon as they occur. At times it is advisable to talk things over, point out how another person wounds others, and start afresh with the air cleared. But a nursed grudge is a viper in the bosom. It is a treasured negative, and you not only let it take away your peace of mind, you also encourage the formation of ulcers and many other ailments which the mind can inflict upon the body. Close that door!

It is wonderful and gratifying to see how the habit of closing the door upon the past becomes one of the greatest of sustaining habits. It helps you take possession of your own mind and condition it for the attainment of any purpose you desire.

Go the extra mile. I have often been asked to give a man something to do that helps him leave resentment behind him; especially where his job and his career are concerned. The best possible action is this: go the extra mile.

Give more service and better service than you are paid for. Find out more about your job and the job above it than you absolutely have to know. Work in a way that makes your job do more than it is expected to do for the organization that employs you.

A young man was an estimator for a large printing firm. He didn't pay much attention to type faces, being content to let the customers go on using the type faces to which they were accustomed. This made his job easier—but, as I pointed out to him, it did nothing to qualify him as a man who really knows his job.

He studied type faces, arrangements of type on a page and other matters which lend effect and even artistry to broadsides and brochures. When his boss received compliments on "the beautiful jobs you turn out," the boss realized what this young man was doing for his firm's reputation. The young man is now an executive of the firm, where before he was scarcely noticed. The young man also has relieved himself of a feeling of bitterness which might, in the end, have resulted in making him an old man with a mean little salary and a mean little soul.

A saleswoman at a dry goods counter had decided that her salary and her small commissions paid her for going through the routine motions of selling what she found on the shelves, and that was that. One day a woman asked her so pleasantly and so positively to look for an item in the depths of the stockroom that she found herself looking; and when she discovered the item, she felt "bigger inside." Thereafter she made a point of suggesting items which were not visible and of putting through special orders even when they resulted in little benefit to herself.

Soon she had a regular clientele. Customers were willing to wait in order to have her serve them. Moreover, her knowledge of her business caused the buyer to rely upon her judgment. She is a buyer now, with a grand career opening before her. She says: "There are two factors that can make you successful; your job and yourself. You are always the most important factor."

Of course you don't have to feel mean and small and imposed upon before you go the extra mile!

A tonic in itself, the willingness to do more than you absolutely must is the hallmark of the big earner, the great leader, the happy and hearty person who day by day builds value into his life.

See yourself on the next step up the ladder, and the next step above that one, and many rewarding steps ahead, and the image takes hold firmly in your mind and gets you going. Should you meet a situation in which your extra efforts are not rewarded, your positive mind finds courage and resourcefulness and you leave the job that's wrong for you—push it back into your past—and find another in which the image becomes real. Where you start never matters so much as where you are going—and it is first within your own mind that you conceive greatly and begin to go.

Again the Supreme Secret has been mentioned in several ways. You may not yet be able to put it into words, but it works more and more strongly in your favor as you read successive chapters of this book.

POINTS TO REMEMBER

1. Your wealth and your peace of mind are strongly connected with each other.
2. Every adversity has within it the seed of an equivalent or a greater benefit.
3. Let go of your past regrets and fights in order to be at peace.

8

LEARN FROM ADVERSITY AND DEFEAT

Throughout this book I've reminded you to look for the seed of an equivalent benefit in every defeat you experience. This isn't always easy when you've suffered a setback, but it is an important part of the science of personal achievement. The time to begin mastering this skill is now, instead of while you're licking your wounds.

Failure and pain are one language through which nature speaks to every living creature, pointing out mistakes. Animals may become timid so that they avoid a threatening situation when it arises again; you must become humble so that you can acquire wisdom and understanding. Realize that the turning point at which you begin to attain success is usually defined by some form of defeat or failure.

With this realization, you need not accept defeat as failure but only as a temporary event that may prove to be a blessing in disguise.

EVERYONE FACES DEFEAT

No one who has attained success has not met with some form of failure comparable with the scope of his or her success. Edison "failed" with more than ten thousand different attempts to create a lightbulb before he hit on the formula that worked. Jonas Salk tried countless different media to cultivate the polio virus for a vaccine before he discovered that monkey brain tissue did the job.

Debbie Fields founded the high-profile Mrs. Fields Cookies chain with a single store and expanded it worldwide very quickly. Too quickly, in fact. The costs of expansion crippled the company, and Fields found herself deeply in debt. She learned that trying to own and run all the stores was simply too much. Now she franchises operations instead of running them herself, and the company is profitable and growing once more.

Defeat should be accepted merely as a test which permits you to discover the nature of your thoughts and their relation to your definite major purpose. Knowing this modifies your reaction to adversity and keeps you striving toward your goal. Defeat is never the same as failure unless and until it has been accepted as such. Emerson said:

> Our strength grows out of our weakness. Not until we are pricked and stung and sorely shot at, awakens the indignation which arms itself with secret forces. A great man is always willing to be little. While he sits on the cushion of advantages he goes to sleep. When he is pushed, tormented, defeated, he has a chance to learn something; he has been put on his wits; on his manhood; he has gained facts; learned from his ignorance; been cured of the insanity of conceit; has got moderation and real skill.

Defeat, however, does not promise the full-blown flower of benefit, only the seed from which some benefit may be coaxed. You must recognize the seed, nurture, and cultivate it by definiteness of purpose; otherwise it will never sprout. Nature looks with disfavor on any attempt to obtain something for nothing,

You need to thank your faults when they are revealed to you because you cannot truly understand them until you have fought them.

ADVERSITY BECOMES A BLESSING

Milo C. Jones operated a small farm in Wisconsin. He was barely subsisting at it when disaster struck: He suffered a paralyzing stroke.

His relatives were so convinced that he was a hopeless invalid that they put him to bed and left him there. Unable to use his body, Jones turned to his mind. Almost immediately he had an idea that was destined to compensate him for his misfortune.

He summoned his relatives together and charged them with planting his entire acreage with corn. That corn would be used to feed a herd of pigs. Those pigs would be slaughtered and turned into sausage.

Within a few years Jones's sausage was being sold in stores all across the nation. You know it as Jones Farm sausage. Milo Jones and his family became wealthier than they had ever dreamed.

This happened because Jones was forced by adversity to turn to a resource he had never really used: his mind. He formed a definite major purpose and a plan for realizing it. He created a mastermind alliance with his family, and with applied faith they carried out the plan that a stroke had brought to a poor farmer.

When defeat overtakes you, don't spend your time counting your losses. Save it to count your gains and assets, and you will realize that they are greater than any loss you have suffered.

You may wonder why Milo C. Jones had to be overcome by a debilitating ailment before he discovered the power of his mind. Others might say that his compensation for that ailment was only financial and therefore not equivalent to his loss of mobility.

But Jones also received spiritual benefits in realizing the power of his mind and the strength of his family. His success, to be sure, did not restore control of his body. But it did give him control of his destiny, which is the highest form of personal achievement. He could have lived out his life in his bed, worrying about himself and his family. Instead he was able to bring them security they would otherwise never have known.

Prolonged illness, like any crippling defeat, often forces us to stop, look, and listen. We learn to understand that still, small voice which speaks to us from within and leads us to take inventory of the factors which have led to defeat and failure in the past.

Again Emerson points the way in these matters:

> A fever, a mutilation, a cruel disappointment, a loss of wealth, a loss of friends, seems [sic] at the moment unpaid loss, and unpayable. But the sure years reveal the deep remedial force that underlies all facts. The death of a dear friend, spouse, brother, lover, which seemed nothing but privation somewhat later assumes the aspect of a guide or genius; for it commonly operates revolutions in our way of life, terminates an epoch of infancy or of youth which was waiting to be closed, breaks up a wonted occupation, or a household, or style of living, allows the formation of new ones more friendly to the growth of character.
>
> It permits or constrains the formation of new acquaintances, and the reception of new influences that prove of first importance to the next years; and the man or

> woman who would have remained a sunny garden flower, with no room for its roots and too much sunshine for its head, by the falling of the walls and the neglect of the gardener is made the banyan of the forest, yielding shade and fruit to wide neighborhoods of man.

Time is relentless in preserving the seed of an equivalent benefit that hides within a defeat. The best time to begin looking for that seed in a new defeat is now. But you can also examine past losses for the seeds they contain. Indeed, sometimes the weight of the loss prevents you from searching at the time. But now, with your increased wisdom and experience, you are ready to examine any loss for the lesson it can teach you.

THE MAJOR CAUSES OF PERSONAL FAILURE

To give you some perspective on the losses you face, I have below listed the most common and powerful causes of failure. When you recognize any that have hampered you, it is important that you do not berate yourself for their presence in your life. Instead you must resolve to do something about them, and do it now!

1. The habit of drifting through life without a definite major purpose
2. Meddlesome curiosity about other people's affairs
3. Inadequate education
4. Lack of self-discipline, manifested as both uncontrolled appetites and indifference to opportunity
5. Lack of ambition
6. Ill health that results from negative thinking and poor diet
7. Unfavorable childhood influences

8. Lack of persistence and follow-through
9. Negative mental attitude
10. Lack of emotional control
11. The desire to get something for nothing
12. Failure to reach decisions promptly and firmly when all the facts needed for the decision are available
13. One or more of the seven basic fears: poverty, criticism, ill health, loss of love, old age, loss of liberty, death
14. Poor selection of a spouse
15. Overcaution or the lack of caution
16. Poor choice of a vocation or occupation
17. Indiscriminate spending of time and money
18. Lack of control over the tongue
19. Intolerance
20. Failure to cooperate with others in a spirit of harmony
21. Disloyalty
22. Lack of vision and imagination
23. Egotism and vanity
24. Desire for revenge
25. Unwillingness to go the extra mile

That's quite a list. But the causes of failure are many, and often you will find more than just one has led to your downfall.

In my youth I founded a magazine in Chicago dedicated to exhorting readers to strive for success. I lacked the capital for this venture, so I entered into a partnership with my printer. The magazine was a success, and even though I had to work long, endless hours, I was happy.

But I was not paying attention. My success threatened another publisher, and without my knowledge he bought out my printer partner and took over my magazine. I was out of work and separated from my labor of love in a most humiliating way,

Many of the above causes for failure were responsible for my defeat. The most important was that I had neglected to cooperate with my partner in a spirit of harmony; I bickered with him often about trivial details of publication. When the opportunity came to be free of me—and to make a profit doing it—he jumped at the chance. My egotism and vanity were responsible for much of this, as were my general lack of caution in business affairs and my sharp tongue.

But—and this is an important "but"—I did manage to find the seed of equivalent benefit by seeing these flaws in my way of doing business. I left Chicago for New York, where I founded a new magazine, one over which I retained control. To achieve this end, I truly had to inspire cooperation in my new business partners, who were risking their money without the power my former partner had kept. I also had to be much more cautious in my business planning since I depended more deeply on my own resources.

The result was a magazine that, within a year, had more than twice the circulation of my previous venture. And it was as a part of my efforts to build the profits of that magazine that I conceived a series of correspondence courses which were the first codification of the science of personal achievement.

I stood at a fork in the road when I was dethroned from my Chicago magazine. I could have given up and returned to the quiet lawyer's job my wife's family urged on me. Instead I recognized the seeds of equivalent benefit in my defeat, and I nurtured that seed beyond my wildest dreams.

THE BENEFITS OF DEFEAT

- Defeat reveals and breaks bad habits, releasing your energies for a fresh start with better habits.
- Defeat supplants vanity and arrogance with humility, paving the way for more harmonious relationships.
- Defeat causes you to take inventory of your assets and liabilities, both physical and spiritual.
- Defeat strengthens your willpower by providing it with a challenge to greater effort.

Bodybuilders know that it isn't enough just to jerk the barbell up; it has to be returned to its original position twice as slowly as it was raised. This principle is known as resistance training; it requires more control and effort than the showy work of actually lifting the weight.

Defeat can be your resistance training. Every time you return to where you started, do it deliberately, concentrating on the process, so that you train yourself to make even stronger and more powerful progress the next time.

YOUR ATTITUDE TOWARD DEFEAT

Again and again I've stressed that your attitude toward defeat is crucial to mastering it. You can see it only as a loss or as a chance for gain.

The negative attitude toward defeat is effectively summarized by Shakespeare in Julius Caesar when the murderer Brutus says:

> There is a tide in the affairs of men,
> Which taken at the flood, leads on to fortune;
> Omitted, all the voyage of their life

> Is bound in shallows and in miseries.
> On such a full sea are we now afloat;
> And we must take the current when it serves,
> Or lose our ventures.

These are the words of a doomed man, a man who seals his doom by failing to recognize that there is never just one chance, never just one tide that leads on to fortune.

The positive attitude is very different. Consider this poem by Walter Malone, entitled "Opportunity":

> They do me wrong who say I come no more,
> When once I knock and fail to find you in;
> For every day I stand outside your door,
> And bid you wake and rise, to fight and win.
>
> Wail not for precious chances passed away;
> Weep not for golden ages on the wane;
> Each night I burn the records of the day;
> At sunrise every soul is born again.
>
> Laugh like a boy at splendors that have sped,
> To vanished joys be blind and deaf and dumb;
> My judgments seal the dead past with its dead,
> But never bind a moment yet to come.

Malone's vision of defeat is the one you will prefer when you have discovered that every defeat carries the seed of an equivalent benefit. Remember, "At sunrise every soul is born again." That rebirth is the opportunity to put defeat behind you.

Fear, self-limitation, and the acceptance of your defeat as final will cause you to be "bound in shallows and in miseries," as Shakespeare suggests. But these things can be overcome by applied faith, a positive mental attitude, and a definite major purpose.

If you accept defeat as an inspiration to try again with renewed confidence and determination, attaining success will be only a matter of time. The secret to this is your positive mental attitude.

Remember, a positive mental attitude attracts success. You need that attraction most when coping with defeat. Redouble your efforts to maintain and build your PMA when adversity strikes, and use your applied faith in yourself and your purpose to put your PMA into action. That is the fundamental lesson in learning from adversity and defeat.

POINTS TO REMEMBER

1. Do not accept defeat as failure but only as a temporary event that may prove to be a blessing in disguise.
2. Instead of focusing on your setbacks, maintain focus on your goal.
3. The major causes of failure and how to change your attitude towards it.

9

THE MASTERY OF POVERTY

Poverty is the result of a negative condition of the mind, which practically every living person experiences at one time or another. It is the first and the most disastrous of the seven basic fears, but it is only a state of mind, and like the other six fears, it is subject to the control of the individual.

The fact that a major portion of all people are born in surroundings of poverty, *accept it as inescapable*, and go with it all through their lives, indicates how potent a factor it is in the lives of people. It may well be that poverty is one of the testing devices with which the Creator separates the weak from the strong, for it is a notable fact that those who master poverty, become rich not only in material things, *but also rich and often wise in spiritual values as well.*

I have observed that men who have mastered poverty invariably have a keen sense of Faith in their ability to master practically everything else which stands in the way of their progress; while those who have accepted poverty as inescapable show signs of weakness in many other directions. In no case have I known anyone who had accepted poverty as unavoidable, who had not failed also to exercise that great Gift of the power to take possession of his own mind-power (as the Creator intended all people should do).

All people go through testing periods throughout their lives, under many circumstances, which clearly disclose whether or not they have accepted and used that Great Gift of exclusive control over their own mind-power. And I have observed that along with this Great Gift from the Infinite go also definite penalties for neglect to embrace and use the Gift, and definite rewards for its recognition and use.

One of the more important rewards for its use consists in complete freedom from the entire seven basic fears and all the lesser fears, with full access to the magic power of FAITH to take the place of these fears.

The penalties for neglect to embrace and use this Great Gift are legion. In addition to all of the seven basic fears, there are many other liabilities not included with these fears. One of the major penalties for failure to use the Great Gift is *the total impossibility of attaining peace of mind.*

Poverty has many merits if and when an individual relates himself to it in a positive mental attitude instead of submitting to it in the false belief that it is unavoidable, or the lazy attitude that it is not worth fighting off. Poverty may be one of the devices with which the Creator forces man to sharpen his wits, arouse his enthusiasm, act on his personal initiative and make a determined fight against the forces which oppose him, in order that he may survive.

Poverty may also be a device of the Creator by which he maneuvers man into a state of mind where he finally *discovers himself from within.* In a great country like the United States of America there is no valid reason for any able-minded person to accept and become bound to slavery through poverty. Here, as nowhere else in the world, is a training ground for personal freedom, which offers every individual the best of all possible opportunities to embrace and use this Great Gift of the *right to pattern his own earthly destiny and attain it.* And here, as nowhere else, has the individual been provided with every conceivable motive for embracing and using the Great Gift. The payoff is so great that the individual may literally "write his own ticket."

The best evidence that Destiny smiles on those who are born to poverty consists in the well-recognized fact that too seldom does an individual who is born to great wealth ever make any worthy contributions to the world which make it a better place for mankind. Many children of very rich people, who never have the benefit of the seasoning influence of poverty or struggle, often grow up "soft" and lacking in the necessary endurance or the motive to make themselves useful.

When fortune does smile upon a person who has great wealth she generally chooses only those who created their wealth through useful service—not those who inherited it or procured it through means which brought injury to others. Fortune definitely frowns upon all ill-gotten wealth, *and often causes it to mysteriously evaporate.*

POVERTY IS A STATE OF MIND

Whether poverty becomes a curse or a blessing depends entirely upon the way the individual relates himself to it. If it is accepted in a spirit of meekness, as an unavoidable handicap, then it becomes just that. If poverty is accepted as a mere challenge to the individual to fight his way through and master, then it becomes a blessing—in fact, one of the great miracles of life. Poverty may become either a stumbling-block or a stepping-stone on which he may rise to whatever heights of achievement he may set his heart upon, depending entirely on his attitude toward it and his *reactions to it.*

Both poverty and riches consist in a state of mind! They follow precisely the pattern the individual creates and visualizes by the dominating thoughts he expresses. Thoughts of poverty attract their material counterpart. Thoughts of riches likewise attract their material counterpart. The law of *harmonious attraction* translates all thoughts into their kindred material counterparts. This great truth explains why the majority of people experience unhappiness and poverty throughout their lives. They allow their minds to fear unhappiness and poverty, and their dominating thoughts are on these circumstances. The law of harmonious attraction takes over and brings them *that which they expect.*

When I was a small boy I heard a very dramatic speech on the subject of poverty which made a lasting impression upon my mind, and I am sure that speech was responsible for my determination to master poverty despite the fact that I had been born in poverty and had never known anything except poverty. The speech came from my stepmother shortly after she came to our home and took over one of the most forlorn, poverty-stricken places I have ever known.

The speech was as follows:

"This place which we call home is a disgrace to all of us and a handicap for our children. We are all able-bodied people and there is no need for us to accept poverty when we know that it is the result of nothing but laziness or indifference.

"If we stay here and accept the conditions under which we now live, our children will grow up and accept these conditions also. I do not like poverty; I have never accepted poverty as my lot, and I shall not accept it now!

"For the moment I do not know what our first step will be in our break for freedom from poverty, but this much I do know—we shall make that break successfully, no matter how long it may take or how many sacrifices we may have to make. I intend that our children shall have the advantage of good educations, *but more than this, I intend that they shall be inspired with the ambition to master poverty.*

"Poverty is a disease which, once it is accepted, becomes a fixation which is hard to shake off.

"It is no disgrace to be born in poverty but it most decidedly is a disgrace to accept this birthright as irrevocable.

"We live in the richest and the greatest country civilization has yet produced. Here opportunity beckons to everyone who has the ambition to recognize and embrace it, and as far as this family is concerned, if opportunity does not beckon to us, *we shall create our own opportunity to escape this sort of life.*

"Poverty is like creeping paralysis! Slowly it destroys the desire for freedom, strips one of the ambition to enjoy better things of life, and undermines personal initiative. Also, it conditions one's mind for the acceptance of myriad fears, including the fear of ill health, the fear of criticism and the fear of physical pain.

"Our children are too young to know the dangers of accepting poverty as their lot, but I shall see to it that they are made conscious of these dangers, and I shall see to it also that they become prosperity conscious, *that they expect prosperity and become willing to pay the price of prosperity."*

I have quoted this speech from memory, but it is substantially what my stepmother said to my father in my presence shortly after they were married. That "first step" in the break from poverty, which she mentioned in her speech, came when my stepmother inspired my father to enter Louisville Dental College and became a dentist, and paid for his training with the life insurance money she received from the death of her first husband.

With the income from that investment in my father, she sent her three children and my younger brother through college and started each of them on the road to mastery of poverty.

As for myself, she was instrumental in placing me in a position where the late Andrew Carnegie gave me an opportunity such as no other author ever received—an opportunity which permitted me to learn from more than five hundred of the top-ranking, successful men who collaborated with me in giving the world a practical philosophy of personal achievement. A philosophy based on the "know-how" of my collaborators, gained from their lifetime experiences.

While it is estimated that my personal contribution to posterity has benefited many millions of people, throughout two-thirds of the world, the credit for this accomplishment really dates back to that historic speech of my stepmother's, in which she disavowed poverty.

We see, therefore, that poverty can be the means of inspiring one to plan and achieve profound objectives. My stepmother did not fear poverty, but she disliked it and refused to accept it. And somehow the Creator seems to favor those who *know precisely what they want and what they do not want.* My stepmother was one of that type. If she had accepted poverty, or had she feared poverty, the lines you are now reading never would have been written.

Poverty is a great experience, but it is something to experience and then master before it breaks the will to be free and independent. The person who has never experienced poverty is to be pitied, perhaps, but the person who has experienced poverty and has accepted it as his lot is more to be pitied, for he has thereby condemned himself to eternal bondage.

Most of the truly great men and women throughout civilization have known poverty, but they experienced it, renounced it, mastered it and made themselves free. Otherwise they never would have become great. Anyone who accepts from life anything he does not want is not free. The Creator has provided everyone with the means of determining very largely his own earthly destiny, which consists in the privilege of freeing himself from those things which are not desirable.

Poverty can be a profound blessing. It can also be a lifelong curse. The determining factor as to which it shall be consists in one's mental attitude toward it. If it is accepted as a challenge to greater effort, it is a blessing. If it is accepted as an unavoidable handicap, then it is an enduring curse.

POINTS TO REMEMBER

1. Poverty is a negative state of mind.
2. The seven basic fears and how to overpower them.
3. Use poverty to discover yourself from within.

10

GROWTH THROUGH STRUGGLE

The necessity for struggle is one of the clever devices through which nature *forces* individuals to expand, develop, progress, and become strong through resistance. Struggle can, and does, become either an ordeal or a magnificent experience through which the individual expresses gratitude for the opportunity to conquer the cause of his struggle.

Life, from birth until death, is literally an unbroken record of an ever increasing variety of struggles, which no individual can avoid.

Mastery of ignorance calls for struggle. Education involves eternal struggle, and every day is commencement day because education is cumulative. It is a lifetime job.

The accumulation of material riches abounds in the necessity for struggle; so much so in fact that many individuals actually kill themselves early in life due to anxiety and overexertion in the effort to acquire more money than they need.

Maintenance of sound physical health calls for eternal struggle with the multifarious enemies of sound health: struggle for food and shelter; struggle for an opportunity to earn a living; struggle to hold a job; struggle to gain recognition in a profession; struggle to keep a business out of bankruptcy.

Look in whatever direction we may, and we find that there

is hardly a circumstance of daily life which does not call for individual struggle in order to survive.

We are forced to recognize that this great universal necessity for struggle must have a definite and useful purpose. That purpose is to force the individual to sharpen his wits, arouse his enthusiasm, build up his spirit of Faith, gain definiteness of purpose, develop his power of will, inspire his faculty of imagination to give him new uses for old ideas and concepts, and *thereby fulfill some unknown mission for which he may have been born.*

Struggle keeps man from going to sleep with self-satisfaction or laziness, and forces him onward and upward in the fulfillment of his mission in life, and he thereby makes his individual contribution to whatever may be the Universal Purpose of mankind on earth.

Strength, both physical and spiritual, is the product of struggle!

"Do the thing," said Emerson, "and you shall have the power."

Meet struggle and master it, says nature, and you shall have *strength and wisdom sufficient for all your needs.*

If you wish a strong arm, says nature, give it systematic use under the weight of a three-pound hammer and soon you will have muscles like bands of steel. If you do not wish a strong arm, says nature, tie it in a sling, take it out of use, and remove the cause for struggle, and its strength will wither and die.

In every form of life, atrophy and death come from idleness! The only thing nature will not tolerate is idleness. Through the necessity for struggle and the Law of Change nature keeps everything throughout the universe in a constant state of ux. Nothing, from the electrons and the protons of matter to the suns and planets which float throughout space, is ever still for a single second. Nature's motto is: Keep moving or perish! There is no halfway ground, no compromise, no exceptions for any reason whatsoever.

And should you doubt that nature intends every individual to keep struggling or perish, observe what takes place with the person who makes his fortune and "retires"—gives up the struggle because he no longer believes it is necessary.

PRINCIPLE OF COSMIC HABIT FORCE

The strongest trees are not those in heavily protected forests, but the trees which stand in open spaces where they are in constant struggle with wind and all the elements of weather.

My grandfather was a wagon maker. In clearing his land for the production of crops, he always left a few oaks standing in the open elds, where they could be toughened by exposure. These he later cut and used for the "fellows" needed in making wagon wheels—timber that could be bent into arc-shaped segments without breaking in the process. He found that trees protected by the forest could not produce the sort of timber he required. It was too soft and brittle because it had not been under the necessity for struggle—the self-same reason why some people are "soft" and unprepared to cope with the resistances of life.

Most people go through life by the line of least resistance in every circumstance where they can make a choice. They do not recognize *that following the line of least resistance makes all rivers, and some men, crooked!*

There may be some pain in most forms of struggle, but nature compensates the individual for the pain in the form of *power and strength and wisdom which come from practical experience.*

While organizing the Science of Success philosophy, I made the revealing discovery that all the more successful leaders, in every calling, in every profession, and every walk of life, had gained their leadership in almost exact ratio to the extent of their struggles in the attainment of their leadership.

I observed, with profound interest, that no man who had not been thoroughly tested by the necessity of struggle, seemed ever to have been chosen as a leader in times of great crises during the interim between the stone age and our present day civilization.

Careful study of the entire record of civilization itself, from the age of the cave man to the present, shows clearly that it is the product of eternal struggle. Yes, struggle definitely is one of the Creator's devices for forcing individuals to respond to the Law of Change in order that the overall plan of the universe may be carried out.

When any individual reconciles himself to the state of mind wherein he is willing to accept largess from the government, instead of supplying his needs through personal initiative, that individual is on the road to decay and spiritual blindness. When a majority of the people of any nation give up their inherited prerogative right to make their own way through struggle, *history shows clearly that the entire nation is in a tailspin of decay that inevitably must end in extinction.*

The individual who not only is willing to live on the public treasury, *but demands that he be fed from it,* is already dead spiritually. The physical body still walks, but it is only an empty shell whose only hope for the future is a funeral. This, of course, has reference only to able-bodied people who quit the struggle because they are too indifferent or too lazy to keep on growing through the Law of Change and the urge for struggle.

For twenty odd years I was forced to struggle in mastering the problems incidental to my work in organizing the world's first practical philosophy of success. First, I was forced to struggle in preparing myself with the necessary knowledge to produce the philosophy. Secondly, I was forced to struggle to maintain myself economically while doing the research necessary to organize the philosophy. Then I met with still greater necessity for struggle while gaining recognition from the world for myself and the philosophy.

Twenty years of struggle without any direct financial compensation is an experience not calculated to give one sustained hope, but it was the price I had to pay for a philosophy which was destined to benefit untold numbers of people, many of whom were not born when I began my work.

Discouraging? Heartbreaking? Not at all, for I recognized from the beginning that out of my struggle would come triumph and victory in proportion to the labors invested in my task. In this hope I have not been disappointed, but I have been overwhelmed with the bountiful manner in which the world has responded and paid me tribute for the long years of struggle that went into my work.

Also, I have gained from my struggle something of still greater and more profound value. It is recognition that through my struggles I *have reached deeply into the spiritual wells of my soul*, and there I have found powers available for every purpose I may desire—powers I never knew I possessed, *and never would have discovered except by the means of struggle!*

Through my struggles I discovered, and learned how to make use of, the magical Eight Princes of Guidance—the unseen friends who administer to all of my physical, financial, and spiritual needs, who work for me while I sleep and while I am awake.

Also, it was through my struggles that the great Law of Cosmic Habitforce (the law that is the fixer of all habits, the comptroller of all natural laws) was revealed to me; the law which led me, at long last, to where I was ready to give the world the benefit of my experiences through struggle.

From my experiences with struggle I discovered that the Creator never singles out an individual for an important service to mankind without first testing him, through struggle, in proportion to the nature of the service he is to render. Thus, through struggle, I learned to interpret the laws, purposes, and working plans of the Creator as they related to me and to mankind in general.

What greater benefits could anyone desire from struggle?

What greater rewards could anyone gain from any other cause?

There is good in all circumstances which touch or influence our lives, whether they be circumstances over which we have complete control or those over which we have no control *except the control of our mental reaction to them.*

As we proceed on our trip, through the chapters to follow, our minds should unfold until we recognize that circumstances which we may regard as unpleasant may be a part of the Creator's overall plan in connection with human destiny on this earth. The major purpose of this chapter is to broaden the mind so it may encompass and envision important facts of life *outside of those which immediately concern* the individual.

Peace of mind is not possible without this capacity for panoramic vision of the entire picture and purpose of life. We must recognize that our individual incarnation, through which we are tossed into this material world without ceremony and without our consent, was for a purpose above and beyond our individual pleasures and desires.

Once we understand this broader purpose of life we become reconciled to the experiences of struggle we must undergo while passing this way, and we accept them as circumstances of opportunity through which we may prepare ourselves for still higher and better planes of existence than the one on which we now dwell.

POINTS TO REMEMBER

1. Struggle is a necessity to become stronger.
2. Struggle makes you contribute to whatever may be your Universal Purpose on earth.
3. Keep moving or perish!

11

PLEASING PERSONALITY

What is an ATTRACTIVE *personality?*

Of course the answer is: *A personality that attracts.* But what *causes* a personality to attract? Let us proceed to find out. *Your* personality is the sum total of your characteristics and appearances which distinguish you from all others. The clothes you wear, the lines in your face, the tone of your voice, the thoughts you think, the character you have developed by those thoughts, all constitute parts of your *personality.*

Whether your *personality* is attractive or not is another matter.

By far the most important part of your *personality* is that which is represented by your character, and is therefore the part that is not visible. The style of your clothes and their appropriateness undoubtedly constitute a very important part of your personality, for it is true that people form first impressions of you from your outward appearance.

Even the manner in which you shake hands forms an important part of your *personality*, and goes a very long way toward attracting or repelling those with whom you shake hands.

This art can be cultivated.

The expression of your eyes also forms an important part of your *personality*, for there are people, and they are more numerous than one might imagine, who can look through your eyes into your heart and see that which is written there by the nature of your most secret thoughts.

The vitality of your body—sometimes called personal magnetism—also constitutes an important part of your *personality.*

HOW TO ATTAIN A PLEASING PERSONALITY

Let us turn our attention to the study of ways and means through which one may develop a *pleasing personality.*

Let us start with the first essential, which is *character.*

Character

For no one may have a *pleasing personality* without the foundation of a sound, positive character. Through the principle of telepathy you "telegraph" the nature of your character to those with whom you come in contact, which is responsible for what you have often called an "intuitive" feeling that the person whom you had just met, but about whom you did not know very much, was not trustworthy.

You may embellish yourself with clothes of the neatest and latest design, and conduct yourself in a most pleasing manner as far as outside appearances go; but if there is greed, and envy, and hatred, and jealousy, and avarice, and selfishness in your heart, you will never *attract* any, except those characters which harmonize with your own. Like attracts like, and you may be sure, therefore, that those who are attracted to you are those whose inward natures parallel your own.

You may embellish yourself with an artificial smile that belies your feelings, and you may practice the art of hand shaking so that you can imitate, perfectly, the hand-shake of the person who is an adept at this art, but, if these outward manifestations of an *attractive personality* lack that vital factor called *earnestness of purpose* they will repel instead of attract.

How, then, may one build *character?*

The first step in character building is rigid *self-discipline-.*

First: Select those whose characters were made up of the qualities which you wish to build into your own character, and then proceed to appropriate these qualities, through the aid of *Autosuggestion.* Create, in your imagination, a council table and gather your characters around it each night, first having written out a clear, concise statement of the particular qualities that you wish to appropriate from each. Then proceed to affirm or suggest to yourself, in outspoken, audible words, that you are developing the desired qualities in yourself. As you do this close your eyes and see, in your imagination, the figures seated around your imaginary table.

Second: Control your thoughts and keep your mind vitalized with thoughts of a positive nature. Let the dominating thought of your mind be a picture of the person that you intend to be: the person *that you are deliberately building,* through this procedure. At least a dozen times a day, when you have a few minutes to yourself, shut your eyes and direct your thoughts to the figures which you have selected to sit at your imaginary council table; and feel, with a *faith* that knows *NO LIMITATION,* that you are actually growing to resemble in character those figures of your choice.

Third: Find at least one person each day, and more if possible, in whom you see some good quality that is worthy of praise, and *praise it.* Remember, however, that this praise must not be in the nature of cheap, insincere flattery; it must be genuine. Speak your words of praise with such earnestness that they will impress those to whom you speak; then watch what happens. You will have rendered those whom you praise a decided benefit of great value to them; and, you will have gone just one more step in the direction of developing the habit of looking for and finding the good qualities in others. I cannot overemphasize the far-reaching effects of this habit of praising, openly and enthusiastically, the good qualities in others; for this habit will soon reward you with a feeling of self-respect and manifestation of gratitude from others, that will modify your entire personality. Here, again, the law of attraction enters, and those whom you praise will see, in you, the qualities that you see in them. Your success in the application of this formula will be in exact proportion to your *faith* in its soundness.

I do not merely believe that it is sound—*I know that it is*—and the reason I *know* is that I have used it successfully and I have also taught others how to use it successfully; therefore, I have a right to promise you that you can use it with equal success.

Furthermore, you can, with the aid of this formula, develop an *attractive personality* so speedily that you will surprise all who know you. The development of such a personality is entirely within your own control, a fact which gives you a tremendous advantage and at the same time places upon you the responsibility if you fail or neglect to exercise your privilege.

No one may hope to become a prominent leader in any noteworthy undertaking without developing the ability to speak with forcefulness that carries conviction. While the salesman may never deliver a public address, he will profit, nevertheless, if he develops the ability to do so, because this ability increases his power to talk convincingly in ordinary conversation.

Let us now summarize the chief factors which enter into the development of an *attractive personality*, as follows:

First: Form the habit of interesting yourself in other people; and make it your business to find their good qualities and speak of them in terms of praise.

Second: Develop the ability to speak with force and conviction, both in your ordinary conversational tones and before public gatherings, where you must use more volume.

Third: Clothe yourself in a style that is becoming to your physical build and the work in which you are engaged.

Fourth: Develop a positive character, through the aid of the formula outlined in this lesson.

Fifth: Learn how to shake hands so that you express warmth of feeling and enthusiasm through this form of greeting.

Sixth: Attract other people to you by first "attracting yourself" to them.

Seventh: Remember that your only limitation, within reason, is the one which YOU set up in YOUR OWN mind.

These seven points cover the most important factors that enter into the development of an *attractive personality,* but it seems hardly necessary to suggest that such a personality will not develop of its own accord. *It will develop, if you submit yourself to the discipline herein described, with a firm determination to transform yourself into the person that you would like to be.*

Remove the chips from your shoulders and quit challenging men to engage you in useless arguments! Remove the smoked glasses through which you see what you believe to be the "blueness" of life and behold the shining sunlight of friendliness in its stead. Throw away your hammer and quit knocking, for surely you must know that the big prizes of life go to the *builders* and not the *destroyers.*

The man who builds a house is an artist; the man who tears it down is a junkman. If you are a person with a *grievance* the world will listen to your vitriolic "ravings," providing it does not "see you coming"; but, if you are a person with a *message* of friendliness and optimism, it will listen because it wishes to do so.

POINTS TO REMEMBER

1. Adopt a personality that attracts.
2. Control your thoughts and keep your mind vitalized with thoughts of a positive nature.
3. Start genuinely praising others.

www.ingramcontent.com/pod-product-compliance
Lightning Source LLC
Chambersburg PA
CBHW021158160426
43194CB00007B/789
* 9 7 8 9 3 5 7 0 2 9 5 8 2 *